A Bag of Rocks

One Woman's attempt at deciphering
the how's and whys of her cancer diagnosis

by

Marie Candiotti

First Edition
Published September 2020

ISBN: 978-1-63649-625-2

PRINTED BY
CADILLAC PRINTING COMPANY, INC.
Since 1921
CADILLAC, MICHIGAN

PART 1

PART II

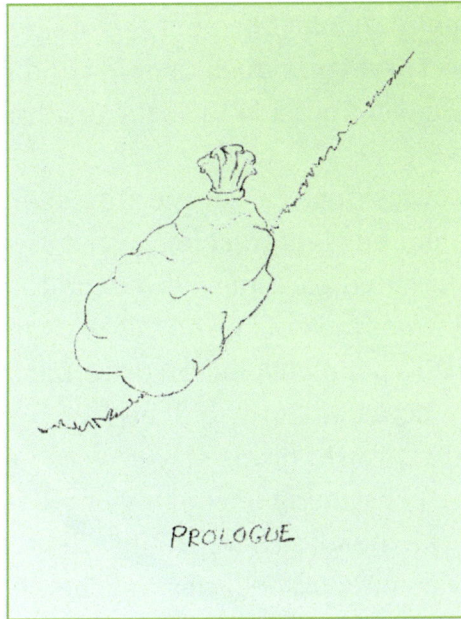

PROLOGUE

PROLOGUE

If I close my eyes, I can transport myself back in time, my lifetime. I can see the small white ranch home I grew up in, on East Main Street on a Saturday morning. Saturday, you may have visions of a leisurely morning, sleeping in, and enjoying a delicious homemade breakfast, nope, not at our house. It was cleaning day. We would dust, sweep, and wipe down all visible surfaces, shake dust rags and small area rugs. If my sister and I were lucky, we could go through our to do list and still have time to watch cartoons before they were over. If you are old enough to remember, or if you're not, let me share with you, that there was a time when cartoons were only aired on a few channels for a few short hours on Saturday morning. There was a very small window of time when we could watch Bugs Bunny outwit Elmer, or the Road Runner outsmart the poor Coyote, so we would be tearing around stirring up dust, opening and slamming the door shut as we went outside to shake dust rags, mops and rugs with wild vigor.

When an occasional car drove into our short gravel driveway it would be of interest because it created a bit of a break in our frenzied cleaning. We would stop to take a quick peek. At times it would be no one we knew as we lived on a dead end and people would turn around after realizing just that. On occasion it would be my Uncle Pete just stopping by to visit. He never stayed very long, and Mom would continue her ironing or cooking or whatever she was doing in the kitchen. They would chat about family members or various personalities and happenings in our small town. There was usually some sighing and shaking of heads. My Uncle would almost always exclaim, "Well, we all have our bag of rocks." They would chuckle then move on to another topic. Now, as a young girl I had no idea what he meant. I liked Uncle Pete all right. He was 17 years older than my Mom and as far as I could tell they got along well even with the age difference.

It wasn't until years later, after Uncle Pete was gone, that I really started to think about just what he meant by that comment. Could it be that we all have burdens we carry around with us? That we throw a rock into our bag every time we have to make a decision? As we all know, life can deal some very unsavory problems to deal with. We also have many forks in the road forcing us to make decisions one way or another. We can knowingly make poor choices yet other times think we are making good choices only to have them turn out to be big mistakes. Did poor choices and big mistakes equal big rocks? This all made sense to me. As years passed, I thought I had accumulated my own bag of rocks. Things I wish I had or hadn't said or done. I should have paid more attention in my High School Spanish class and maybe kept in touch with the good friends that had helped me get through those painful and awkward years.

I wish I had paid more attention in all my classes in College. I should have spent more time with my Dad and kept in touch with my Great Aunt Edith.

I truly should have appreciated my youth more and I really wish I had repaired my red VW Bug instead of selling it. My bag of rocks seemed reasonable for my age. Then I was diagnosed with Ovarian Cancer. Overnight my bag of rocks turned into a wheelbarrow full of boulders. Is this just one of those unsavory hands that life had dealt me, or had I been making poor choices thru out my life?   I try to follow the golden rule. I followed the so -called experts advice on living a healthy life: I didn't smoke or drink I exercised every day and ate a clean mostly plant based diet.

I had cut back on meat long ago and hadn't eaten red meat in over 30 years, not for my health but mainly due to the horribly inhumane way our livestock are raised and treated. Attention to diet and exercise seemed to work for other people so why not for me?

Side note: Why do we abuse and beat the kind and intelligent farm animals then kill and eat them? We are able to obtain all our nutritional needs from other sources and although the jury is still out: from a land usage perspective, pollution run off and human health why not stick to plants?

After several agonizing months I realized I had done nothing to deserve this- nothing to earn these very heavy rocks. This was just not fair. What mistake was I to learn from? I had believed our collection of rocks should help us be better people if we chose to learn from it. Did I have it all wrong? My journey with cancer began in total confusion. Not only did I not understand how living a healthy life had led me to a diseased state but my whole bag of rocks concept was turned around.

It was like a roller coaster ride minus the fun. I was screaming out of desperation not from the thrill. I have to admit I am one of the lucky ones. Not only have I survived but I had incredible care from the diagnosis on, receiving expertise from outstanding Doctors in both Western and Eastern medicinal practices. I also had the chance to see just how very special and rare my family is. Everyone was there for me every step of the way. Helping me to physically, and mentally, move from active disease to a remission state.

Thanks to my husband's employment I also had complete health insurance, something many people in this country do not have. I felt guilty that I was able to receive all treatments needed with no financial burden. Many Americans do not because they cannot afford health insurance or have no savings account, which leaves their family bankrupt. We are suddenly faced with huge life altering decisions both for ourselves, and families. When diagnosed with cancer, you begin to look at your life differently, from a different angle so to speak. For me, one thing didn't change; I still felt part of an intertwined magnificent energy force. Some may call it god, but whatever it is, it's something magnificent that cannot fit into short stories or parables, let alone into one single religion. Just look at the planet we live on. Every living life form has been given all that is needed to survive: air, water, and fertile soil, all in an ever encompassing revolving globe. Every life form, no matter how large or small is connected in some way on this planet. As I gaze skyward, I am able to see only a portion of our own galaxy, but I know there are many more surrounding us. I know how life on earth completely relies on the other planets like the sun and the moon, and I can only believe that in other galaxies such relationships must also exist. To be connected, with all that is around us gives me a sense of belonging, comfort, and strength. As taken from Carl Sagan's book The Cosmic Connection (published 1973; Chapter 26, pages 189-190), "The nitrogen in our DNA, the calcium in our teeth, the iron in our blood, the carbon in our apple pies were all made in the interiors of collapsing stars. We are made of Star stuff."

This book is my story. I have gathered information and written down my personal experience and thoughts on living with cancer. I'd like to thank my sister for drawing all the pictures. I hope you will find new insights, hope, a few chuckles, and perhaps a new perspective.

My childhood home, 1960

Uncle Pete in his younger years

9

CHAPTER 1

PART 1

LOOKING FOR ANSWERS

LOOKING FOR ANSWERS

"A woman is like a tea bag; you can't tell how strong she is
until you put her in hot water"
-Eleanor Roosevelt

As I think back on this crazy experience, many questions bubble up. They usually wake me at night as I lie in bed, thinking about the day ahead, or the day I just bungled thru. Then I weave my way back to my situation at hand: fighting cancer cells. What did I do wrong? Could I have caught it earlier, how did I miss the signs? I try to practice a yoga breath and let the thoughts flow in front of me and dissipate into the night. Sometimes it worked sometimes not. During my treatment, those questions were always popping up, especially Thursday nights, the night before my chemotherapy treatment. I would replay everything, which, if I were talking to a shrink, would be a good thing. The problem was I had no one sitting in a chair next to me telling me I was normal, that I was ok, that everything will turn out fine.

My symptoms had been vague, and when I looked them up on WEB MD, as most of us now do-self diagnose-they were symptoms of many conditions. I just felt frumpy at first. I knew I didn't feel normal but putting my symptoms into words was hard. I never was a person that ran to the Doctor if something felt off. My symptoms would usually go away in a day or so. The doctor's waiting room would always be filled with people who were 'really sick' and I always felt I was filling a time slot that someone else who was worse off should have. Besides, what do you say? Hi, I'm just not feeling well? Looking back the signs were starting to show but who the heck could read them? Certainly not thick headed me.

One of the first signs I didn't pick up on was low iron. I always had been a great blood donor by always showing up to donate blood at various blood drives. It's a great mini checkup: blood pressure, pulse, body temperature, and iron level. On one particular trip before my diagnosis I was turned away for low iron! This was a real blow to my ego. They gave me a nice American Red Cross sticker to put on my coat that read: "I tried" and I slunk out the back door. I wrote it off thinking I was just stressed and would try to relax more and eat more raisins dipped in dark chocolate.

I was and always have been very active, teaching fitness for over 30 years. I had run 5K's, 10K's, and even a marathon in Hawaii with my husband Lou. Prior to my diagnosis I was instructing Pilates to my favorite Pilates class 3 times a week and was also the Fitness Specialist for a healthy family living program at the local hospital, not to mention walking two dogs daily.

I would always feel better after a class or after a walk with the dogs. Movement had always been good medicine for me. Our bodies are meant to be active and not slumped in a lazy boy all day. There is nothing like getting the body's circulation pumping to get rid of the aches and pains one might have.

I began to not feel well after I ate, and so I was eating less and less. This didn't bother me too much. After all, like most of us I could lose a few pounds. What became worrisome was that I couldn't totally empty my bladder. That was a puzzler, but these days there is so much hype around stress, I figured that must be it! 2016 was a stressful election year, I was not happy with the outcome, nor did I like how the whole campaigning year had gone.

I found myself getting really worked up into a lather. I know politics has never been exactly on the up and up...ever, but I kept wondering where was any respect for our fellow human beings? When did poor 6th grade behavior become acceptable? I was very worried about the health of our planet and the total disregard for any life form. It appeared listening skills and common sense had gone by way of the Dodo bird. In addition to that, I had turned 60 and was taking a close look at my life. Where had the time gone?

When I finally did call my doctor, I was given an appointment with one of the newer physicians in the practice. I was very happy. I liked her. We discussed having a colonoscopy, a mammogram, and my mother who was in her 90's and had never been on any medications. Then we got to the real reason I came. Oh yes, my vague symptoms.

13

This didn't seem to faze her a bit and she began her search by ordering a scope. And so it began. After the scope (which found no real problem) I visited 2 gynecologists, as well as urologist, not to mention a few visits to urgent care and the ER. I had been scheduled for more tests when I just couldn't stand it anymore. I had been catheterized and continued to be, along with experiencing more pelvic exams than I would ever wish on an enemy. I was very tired and uncomfortable. My exercise had begun to be more difficult jumping jacks especially, and although I was now able to empty my bladder with help, I still had a full feeling that never went away. I had lost weight, yet my pants felt tight around my waist. Looking back now, I believe that if I hadn't lived such an active lifestyle, we may not have caught my cancer in time.

After seeing all these specialists, my husband Lou and I returned to my new family physician, who at a loss as to just exactly what was going on, sent us to the ER. This was a lifesaver; we had more tests run and did not have to wait the usual 2 to 4 weeks.

It was there that I received the news. They ushered us into a private emergency room, where the doctor had ordered a cat scan of my abdominal area. After drinking a glass of horrible liquid every half hour Lou and I sat listening to the lively activities in the hallway and watching the series 'Bones' on TV. The door opened. Three white coats invaded the room with solemn faces. I had Ovarian Cancer. Wait. What? I thought they must have walked into the wrong room. I was expecting an explanation to my symptoms, but I did not like this one. I sat staring at the picture they were drawing on the large white board in the room. A primitive drawing of where my tumor was, as well as other areas that were in question. Cancer. Stage Three. Lou lowered his head into his hands and tears filled his eyes. He had worked in the ER when he was a student and had worked in the health field all his adult years.

This was something he watched other families go thru not ours. Although I heard what they were saying, I couldn't absorb it all and really didn't want to hear the horrible possibilities or statistics of survival.

My brain seemed to have switched to another frequency. I couldn't absorb what they were telling me. I simply couldn't take it in. I shut their voices out. Could I really be this sick? They weren't going to send me to the pharmacy to fill a prescription or send me home to get some rest. They were telling me my life could be over very soon as there is no cure for cancer. I wasn't ready to become a sad statistic. I put on my brave face and decided I was going to listen and follow their plan as well as do what I could do on my own to somehow become disease free.

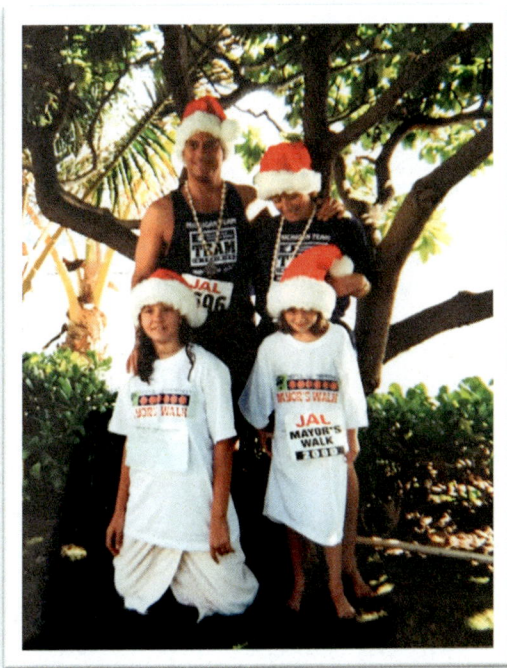

Leukemia Lymphoma Marathon 2000
in Hawaii

CHAPTER 2

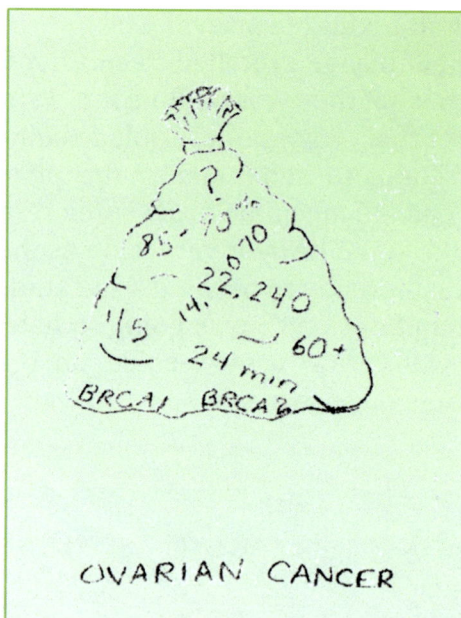

OVARIAN CANCER

OVARIAN CANCER

"Sometimes you win, sometimes you learn"

J. Maxwell

After being given a diagnosis like cancer, some folks want to stick their heads into the ground hoping it will all disappear. Others throw themselves into research mode and learn all they can about the disease. I don't think either one is right or wrong, it's just our own personal way of dealing with the situation. I felt like throwing every single rock that had just been dropped into my lousy bag at anything that moved. We were referred from the ER to an Oncology Practice. First step was to meet with their Nurse Navigator. This is a very specialized Nurse who is familiar with the disease and

16

treatment and works closely with you and your Doctor. My Navigator drove from Ann Arbor to Brighton to meet with my youngest daughter, Ellie, Lou, and me on a Saturday (prior to my first appointment). She continued to help and inform us every step of the way. We walked away with a full folder (in hand) of printed material, our heads spinning with information and intellectually prepared for the first appointment with the Oncologist. Our Nurse Navigator constantly went out of her way to answer any and all questions I, or my family had, whether it was about a missing requisition, a question about a medication or prescription or about the treatments I was receiving.

The next day we called our oldest daughter, Katie, to give her the news. She was living in New York City. How do you tell someone you love this kind of news? We decided to simply stick to the facts at least the few we knew at that time. With today's incredible technology we were able to Face Time her. She could see us, and we could see her. Body language and facial expressions are so important in communication especially with this type of news. It was hard having her so far away, but Lou called her whenever a procedure or test was done to keep her up to speed. It was all so new and scary. It felt as though I had taken a wrong turn hiking leaving a beautiful secure trail in the woods, to a swinging bridge over a river of alligators.

We had a stack of papers and pamphlets that continued to grow. They covered pretty much the whole gambit. It gave information on the research, medications, statistics, and history of cancer. It even told us the color that represented ovarian cancer (teal). We however chose purple to be our team color and wore it to all appointments and infusions. We began to dig into the pile of information. I learned that all cells found in almost every part of the body has the ability to become cancerous. All cancer cells also have the ability to spread throughout the body.

This was pretty unsettling news, because as much as we know about cancer cells, we are still unable to tell for certain why these cells develop or multiply.

There are three types of ovarian tumors. Epithelial tumors (these cells cover the outer surface of the ovary), germ cell tumors (cells that produce eggs), and stromal tumors (structural tissue cells). 85%-90% of ovarian cancers are epithelial. This was the type of tumor I had. Here are some more statistics for you: ovarian cancer is the number one cause of gynecologic deaths in the United States. It's the fifth cause of cancer-related deaths in women and eleventh most common cancer in women. 22,240 new cases were diagnosed in 2018. 50% affecting those at least 60 years old. Yep, that would be me; I just walked in the door to my 6th decade in 2017.

Every 24 minutes another woman is diagnosed with ovarian cancer. This statistic really hits home. I believe it's because I replay receiving my news in the ER that cold February evening, totally blindsided, as many women are. One in seventy nine women will develop ovarian cancer in their lifetime. It was estimated in 2018 14,070 women will die from this disease. Although most research today is in breast cancer, research with ovarian cancer is ongoing.

I searched the information for symptoms, thinking what did I miss? This is what I could find: symptoms may include a discharge from the vagina, pain or pressure in the pelvic/abdominal area, vaginal bleeding, back pain, having to pass urine very often and/or bloating. I only had one of the listed symptoms, I had problems urinating. I later found this was due to the fluid buildup in my abdominal area. Of course looking back I am able to put the pieces together, and say ah, yes! However, at the time, nothing really made sense.

Other factors the medical world uses to diagnose ovarian cancer include: past difficulty getting pregnant or trouble giving birth, Eastern European Jewish background, a history of breast, uterine or colorectal cancers, endometriosis (a painful disorder where tissue that normally grows inside your uterus grows on the outside), a family history of ovarian cancer, middle-aged or older, and finally, a positive blood test for BRCA1 or BRCA2. These are genetic blood tests that a doctor may order and that may not be paid for by your health insurance. We went back and forth with our insurance company after I received the genetic counseling and blood work. We were told we were covered, then not covered, and received the bill...ouch$$$!! My Oncologist called the insurance company to end the dispute and the back and forth ended. They paid, thank goodness.

Most ovarian cancer cases are not detected until the third or fourth stage. I, along with thousands of other women, don't fit into any of the factors or early signs. Some are a clear 'no' as in my case. No one in my family had cancer. I'm not of Jewish descent. I never had endometriosis and didn't test positive for BRCA.

Today there are no true screening tests for ovarian cancer. It is extremely hard to detect early on. A yearly Pap test with your gynecologist screens for cervical cancer. A mammogram will detect breast cancer. A colonoscopy will detect colon cancer. So ladies, we are out there alone on our flotation devices trying to figure out what our bodies are telling us. I believe many times intuition tries to tell us something, but we squash it. "I'm too busy to be sick", "I'll feel better tomorrow", "I am still able to get thru my day without stopping, and therefore I simply can't be too sick."
So take it from a 'Squash Master', listen to that little voice and be persistent, keep asking questions until you get an answer and a plan for relief.

CHAPTER 3

THE GAME PLAN

"Perseverance is not a long race: it is many short races,
one after the other"
-Walter Elliot

It felt like after my diagnosis I jumped with both feet into a supersized tornado. The ER had immediately referred me to an Oncologist Office.

There was no time to think about what to do. I had watched as friends and friends of friends had been diagnosed with various cancers and had thought I couldn't do what they did- go thru what they went thru with no guarantee of becoming well again. However, after our first meeting with the Oncologists, we were on our way to drain the fluid buildup in my abdomen, insert a port in my chest and the first Chemotherapy Treatment, all within a week. Every procedure was foreign to me; the technicians and medical staff were wonderful. They whizzed me from room to room doing their thing with total confidence, and most had a smile.

I set my game face on again and headed into a procedure where they drain the abdominal area. In medical terms it's called an abdominal paracentesis or an ascetic tap. This procedure relieves symptoms in 9 out of 10 people. This sounded horrible to me. After the usual question and answer period, where they make sure you are you and they are going to do the correct procedure on you, I was wheeled into a room with all kinds of strange and unknown shiny equipment. The staff filled me in every step of the way. How they will simply drain the fluid and send me on my way. Humm, easy for them to say, but that is exactly what happened. They numbed a small area on my abdomen and inserted a long needle. Over 7 pounds of fluid slowly drained into a jug, which sat on the table next to my bed. We were engaged in conversation the entire time and although I enjoyed our conversation I was horrified as I watched the creamy fluid fill the jugs. I knew this fluid would tell the Doctors what type of cancer or cancers I had. Would they only find ovarian cancer cells, or would the liquid contain multiple types of cancer cells, which would make the treatment more difficult. The technicians told me that the amount of fluid they had drawn out was not bad. They had drained much more out of other individuals. I was also informed that in many cases patients would have to return thru out their treatment to repeat the procedure. This was supposed to put my mind at ease? I silently promised my body I would do everything I could to avoid returning.

Without stopping the momentum we moved on to the next procedure. I had a port inserted into my chest the following Wednesday. In some patients, ports are inserted to avoid taking the chance of collapsing veins. Ports can be placed in various locations on the body. Basically an incision is made and a tube inserted into a vein which is attached to a hard round disc like object which sits just under the surface of the skin. This gives medical staff access to a vein for blood draws and or chemotherapy treatments. I hadn't a collapsed vein, but it was always good to have a backup. To demonstrate just how foreign this world was to me I kept calling the port a portal. For those of you who are Harry Potter fans I'm sure you totally understand the mix up. For those of you who are not, a portal, in J.K. Rowling's children's book series is an object, which the characters grab onto and are then magically transported from one location to another.

No one corrected me until as I lay on the gurney answering my intake questions, I referred to the port as a portal and the nurse stopped, turned, and gave me a funny look and asked,

"You mean Port?" I then realized my mistake and gave a quick explanation. We both laughed and joked that we would both like to grab that portal and transport out of there.

The procedure went well. The staff filled the room and the Doctor worked his magic as we all discussed kids and parenthood. When they wheeled me out of the room and instructed me to change back into my street clothes, I looked down at the bandage covering the port. I couldn't feel it, but I could see it. There was now a small object lying just beneath the skin, attached to a vein. Incredible.

CHAPTER 4

THE BIG GUNS

THE BIG GUNS

"If we all did the things we are capable of doing,
We would literally astound ourselves."
Thomas Edison

After all the blood work, many tests, and procedures it was time for my first chemotherapy session. The treatment plan was in place, chemotherapy, and surgery, followed by more chemotherapy. My family by my side I began the daunting journey.

Friday, February 17, 2017 Lou and I gathered paperwork, and things we thought we might need for the day and hit the road. It was dark and cold outside. Our minds were going a mile a minute and our hearts were pounding. Getting to the hospital was no easy task as we had 12 miles of construction to maneuver thru. South bound 23 was and had been a mess for years. It had not been updated for decades (and I mean decades) and was not handling the growing population and vehicles that commuted the tired pavement to and from Ann Arbor. It was now getting a much needed face lift, and we were hitting it at rush hour. Oh joy. I always worry about the road workers in yellow. There they are just doing their jobs and folks are rushing past them eating, putting on make-up and of course doing what they do on their cell phones at the same time driving a vehicle that could kill all life forms. This road project had already been a great source of commuting stress for several months. This morning it seemed to intensify. With a sigh of relief we pulled into parking lot Q. I glanced at the huge medical building. Every light was on, behind the windows medical and support staff were all doing their thing. We held hands and headed across the quiet parking lot and thru the sliding doors.

Our first stop was at the Oncologist office. I was ushered into an exam room where I had yet another pelvic exam then moved on to a meeting room where we all sat at a large table: my Nurse Navigator, two Doctors, Lou and myself. We reviewed my case and they answered a few more questions. From the office we took a long hike to radiology, where I had a baseline chest X-ray. After the x-ray, the technician walked me to the changing room. There stood an obviously overwhelmed and frustrated woman trying to open her locker. Having worked in recreation centers and fitness gyms for over 30 years I knew a thing or two about stuck lockers, so I re-knotted the ties on my size XXL designer hospital gown and leaned in. After a few kicks, palm punches and grunting, we were able to retrieve her belongings. I was happy to be of assistance with something that I was familiar with as it took my mind off the rotten reason I was there. It was then another long hike down another long hallway to the laboratory, where the phlebotomist made several attempts to draw my blood. My poor vein was just not having it. After a few more jabs my arm began to look like an oil painting gone terribly wrong. She gave up, wrapped the area with gauze and sent me on my way with the understanding the infusion nurse would make the draw before my treatment. I began to sweat as we took the long hallway towards my first chemotherapy treatment. I had hoped I had applied deodorant before we left home, but I just couldn't remember.

We met our nurse who was incredible and chock full of helpful facts and tidbits. We all became fast friends in the 8 hours plus we spent together. Because it was my first treatment, we had our own room with free run of the small kitchen and a bathroom next door. The nurse first accessed my port and drew my blood like a pro. I learned as treatments went on some professionals could access the port without you feeling even a prick, others not so much.

My treatment plan was to consist of an infusion session every week (which ended up being on Friday). Paclitaxel, (Taxel for short) the first week, followed by two weeks of Carboplatin. This cycle of 3 weeks was considered one full treatment. Paclitaxel, the toughest drug, was on the menu today. Prior to receiving the actual chemotherapy drugs each week, pre-treatment drugs are administered. My port was accessed, and an IV bag was hung. Timing it perfectly my nurse then infused the IV drip with the pre-medications, each time explaining what she was adding to the drip and why. The pre-medications included Benadryl, an antihistamine, Reglan/Famotidine, antiflux drugs, Decadron a steroid, as well as Aloxi and Emend both anti-nausea medications. Finally it was time for the big guns, Taxel. Lou was by my side the whole time. At one point he ran to the cafeteria (he really did need a break!) and picked up a sandwich on delicious homemade bread (my weakness) as well as a huge chocolate chip cookie (another weakness). As the day continued, I had a reaction on two different occasions during that first treatment. Because the staff had been so clear in their description I spoke up as soon as I felt a very strange and warm feeling rising up my body. All of a sudden, I felt as though I was sinking into a very warm puddle of thick muddy water, bum first. By catching it in time we were able to continue the treatment. It did, however, add over an hour to our stay, as we had to stop the treatment and wait 30 minutes each time before continuing on. This added another layer of fear to my already heightened level of anxiety. Was this going to occur every time I came in for an infusion? Why was I having this reaction? Were my pre medications not working? Would this have an effect on the treatments ability to treat the cancer? Only time would tell.

We were on the road for home a little after 6:00 p.m. Rush hour again! Traffic was crazy and it seemed like it took us forever to arrive at our exit. Making a stop at the CVS store we picked up what appeared to me, the entire pharmacy. I have never been a Big Pharmacy fan and I looked with dismay at the many bags full of drugs. How will I keep them all straight? Finally we walked into a warm and lighted house. The dogs greeted us with great enthusiasm, and even the cat sat a short distance from the door and allowed us to pat her head. Ellie had sandwiches and homemade cookies waiting for us, which she served up after we changed our clothes and put on our slippers.

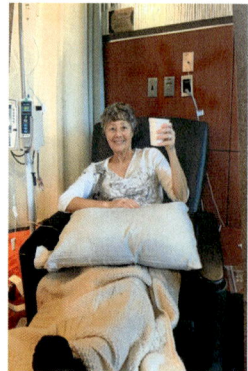

Early treatment (with hair)

What a day. The long, draining, exhausting day. It was over. Only 17 treatments, one surgery, and 22 weeks left to go.

26

CHAPTER 5

THE MANY ROADS

Every head must do his own thinking

African Proverb

I was very concerned about all the bottles of medications that now covered our entire bathroom counter. I felt it was a long shot but wondered if my Oncologist would help me navigate off the pill trail. You know the pill trail: first you take pills for pain and or nausea, caused by the chemotherapy drugs. Then you take pills to counteract those pills that may cause constipation or diarrhea. Then you take pills that may alleviate any other side effects the last round of pills may have caused to your system. It all sounded like a total train wreck to me. In our conversation my Oncologist warned me to stay away from the IV Clinics and various non-mainstream extreme treatments and super doses of anything available today as some of these practices could actually interfere with the Chemotherapy I was receiving. She then handed over a business card of a Chinese Doctor who happened to have an office just down the street from the Hospital. He combined acupuncture with cupping and herbal remedies. Some of her present and previous patients had worked with this Dr. as they received chemotherapy or radiation. I was very glad my Oncologist was open to the two worlds of Western and Eastern Medicine working together because many do not. Many feel anything outside their training is 'voodoo medicine'.

Doctors here in the United States have a traditional training of acute care, which usually involves drugs, surgery, and more drugs. Period. Many have little knowledge of integrative medicine, which means treating the whole person before, during, and after an illness. Today there are more physicians who are going beyond their traditional training and looking at diet, lifestyle, spirituality, and ancient medicine. Many are beginning to see they must treat the entire human being. They see their patient's care involves more than just treating the disease, but also healing the body and mind.

While growing up my family were always pretty healthy (this may be due to a good gene pool). I have always believed in looking at all possibilities before taking a drug. I don't remember anyone going to the doctor very often, or anyone on any medication for that matter. Growing up our medicine cabinet consisted of all over the counter medications. When we caught colds, we gargled with salt water, took naps, smeared Vicks on our chest, and ate chicken noodle soup. Thank goodness no one suffered from depression or a chronic condition. We ate well and went to bed early. The whole family camped, played, hiked, and ice-skated outside together getting plenty of fresh air, sunshine, and healthy doses of laughter. There were times we would laugh so hard we wouldn't be able to utter a word or catch our breath! Growing up we had no battles over screen time, or the car. We only had one TV with just a handful of channels. This gave us plenty of time to use our imaginations and the great out of doors to entertain ourselves. Like many families in the 60's we only had one automobile. My Dad drove it every day to work. My sister and I walked or rode our bikes to school or to run errands for Mom.

I believe this lifestyle helped to make and keep me healthy as I grew up. A combination of healthy family connections, good food, movement, and exposure to the out of doors made for a good recipe. Many professionals share this four -pillar philosophy.

Dr. Rangan Chatterjee is one such professional. After a personal health scare with his young son, this British Doctor began to research functional medicine. This is a whole person approach that uncovers the true root of a disease. He believes in order for you to attain true health you must pay attention to four areas of your life, whole food, daily movement, solid sleep, and the ability to relax. Dr. Chatterjee is able to share his view on a BBC television series "Doctor in the House", as well as via a podcast "Feel Better, Live More". He has also written a book 'How to Make Disease Disappear".

Dr. Mimi Guarneri is another physician who looks outside the normal Western world's medicinal circle. She is the founder of the Scripps Center for Integrative Medicine in California. She is board certified in cardiology, internal medicine, nuclear medicine, and holistic medicine. She is a member of the American college of Cardiology, as well as a Diplomat of the American Board of Integrative Holistic Medicine. Dr. Guarneri describes integrative holistic medicine as a model of care where not just symptoms are treated. The true underlying problem is uncovered by using many medicinal traditions used around the world. It's not alternative medicine where you move away from mainstream practices. Instead, combining many schools of thought. So you may change your diet to one that is more plant based, begin to practice some type of gentle exercise, receive Eastern treatments, yet at the same time, work with Western physicians. I decided to do just that. I walked everyday 30-60 minutes, continued to teach Pilates and practice hot yoga. My diet was pretty much plant based before, but I became stricter and eliminating all processed foods, sugar, and caffeine. I received cupping and acupuncture treatments as well as chemotherapy every week. Dr. Guarneri believes that when it comes to the prevention and treatment of disease, nature provides the best solutions.

This next paragraph is taken from 'The Science of Natural Healing'. "Think of yourself as a tree that has a few health challenges. Think about the soil in which you live. You might label some of the leaves of your tree depression, diabetes, high cholesterol, heartburn" (insert your condition) "some people have many sick leaves. Imagine that the trunk of your tree is your genes-your genetic make-up. Then, think about what makes up the soil because that determines whether you have healthy or sick fruit is a very special interaction between your genes and your environment, and the soil is the environment in which you live." She emphasizes the importance of eating healthy plant based foods, exercise, the support of family or individuals around you, as well as living on a healthy planet.

Dr. Guarneri has been quoted in the Yoga Journal, Whole Living: Body and Soul in balance, Trustee Magazine, and WebMD the Magazine. I especially enjoyed the lecture series available thru the Great Courses. (www.thegreatcourses.com) Although she began as a cardiologist, she addressed many diseases and living a healthy lifestyle that benefits everyone. I would listen to the CD as I commuted in my car.

I felt it empowered me. I felt even though I had this horrible diagnosis, I could do something. I could also practice self - care. This is a popular term these days if you look on social media, used to describe a one-time bubble bath or pedicure but that behavior actually misses the mark. Self- care is all about making lifelong healthy habits. It may have you sticking to a budget if you become stressed over your finances or not eating certain foods should you, after eating them, feel bloated or have heartburn or taking a nap or going to bed early when you're tired. It isn't a one-time pampering activity you post photos of on Facebook. Integrative psychiatrist Henry Emmons, MD explained in the September 2019 issue of Experience Life Magazine; "When you've been in a less healthy state, you have created a certain homeostasis. Things are the way they are and even changing for the better can feel uncomfortable..." So self-care can actually be difficult and was for me as I was used to being on the go all the time.

Not only are many physicians expanding their knowledge, hospitals are too. Cancer patients are now offered Yoga classes, massage services as well as consultations with Registered Dietitians. My Oncologist suggested a prescription of medical marijuana for nausea should I need it. All of these services, just a few years ago would never have been offered, and believed to have had no benefits to any patient.

The argument continues between the two worlds. There are those who want to see only 21 Century medicine, grounded in the most recent research used, and other practitioners who feel tried and true treatments that have worked in the past should continue to be shared. My question is this: why not look at what has benefited thousands of people for hundreds of years, and combine this knowledge with the new findings of today? By combining the two worlds we will create the best possible treatments for all patients everywhere.

My Dad
and
sister
playing
around

Our family camper, 1960-1

CHAPTER 6

MESSAGE FROM PAST

A Message From The Past

"And once the storm is over,
you won't remember how you made it through,
how you managed to survive. You won't even be sure whether
the storm is really over. But one thing is certain,
when you come out of the storm,
you won't be the same person who walked in"
Haruki Murakami

There are many doctors and hospitals today around the world that are combining global medicinal ideas and practices. However I would like to go back in time a bit.

Although I only know of this Doctor from stories, I have heard my Mom and Dad tell as well as a few references to him in various books, I feel it is very fitting to share how he touched my life.   He was a Dutch Doctor who was in the wrong place at the wrong time during WWII. His name was Dr. Henri Hekking.

Dr. Hekking was born on February 13, 1903 on the Island of Java, an Island of Indonesia. His Grandmother was a master herbalist. She had a large garden on the outskirts of the jungle filled with a wide variety of vegetables, many plants, and herbs.   It was because of her, Henri decided to be a Doctor. He would watch her care for the people of the Island with attentive listening skills and using what she grew in her garden to treat them.

Years later, Henri graduated from Medical School earning a Medical Degree thru the University of Leiden under a grant provided by the Royal Dutch Army in exchange for 10 years of service. He specialized in Jungle diseases. Henri learned early on not to bring up what his Grandmother had taught, as most Doctors at that time felt people who used herbs to treat patients were just one step above what they called Snake Oil Salesmen here in the United States. After many years of study, and many moves, Dr. Hekking's world, like so many at that time came crashing down. He was taken prisoner by the Japanese. In deplorable conditions he found himself using a combination of his knowledge he gained from his Grandmother, his formal education and the psychology of healing to help save the lives of many a POW. He truly was Amazing.

The 2nd Battalion 131st Field Artillery otherwise known as The Lost Battalion along with thousands of allied soldiers and native civilians were captured and used as slave labor to build the Thailand-Burma/Death Railroad through the jungle.   My father was one of those soldiers. "Torture, disease, starvation, beatings, and exhaustion claimed many lives" quote taken from 'In Loving Memory', found at the U of M Bentley Museum in Ann Arbor Michigan.

It was at this time my Father met Dr. Hekking. He would take his advice and was forever thankful for his knowledge. Dr. Hekking never received any American Red Cross medical supplies let alone rations as the Japanese intercepted all shipments intended for the POW's. Instead, he used his knowledge of plants such as Cephaelis Ipecacuanta to treat dysentery, maggots and 'scraping' to heal tropical ulcers. He used countless remedies from the very jungle where they were held captive.

"Some of Dr. Hekking's treatments were as old as time itself, yet so far advanced that medical researchers are just now beginning to prove the efficacy of what he knew and practiced even before World War II" (Taken from 'Last Man Out' by H. Robert Charles.).

My Dad survived thanks to pure determination and Dr. Hekking's lessons. Returning home he married my mom, Doris Barnes, started a good job and built that little white ranch on East Main Street. They had two lovely daughters, my sister and myself, but his transition home was far from smooth. It was extremely difficult to say the least. His once strong, young body had endured hard physical labor in the heat of the jungle with only small servings of dirty watered down rice seven days a week for almost four years. The aftereffects of inhumane mental and physical abuse haunted him long after his return home. Dad, just like many who return from war suffered flashbacks. It didn't help that the United Sates downplayed their abuse at the hands of the Japanese, and many of the men including my Dad, simply could not or would not talk about the years of inhumane treatment.

My Father had been starved, and as a result his stomach lining was basically non- existent and although he had returned, and a variety of healthy food was available he couldn't keep much of anything down. He continued to lose weight and the Doctors were at a loss as to what to do. One day my Dad ran into a local farmer and he told him to stop by his farm to pick up a few quarts of goats milk, that it just might help Dad put on a few pounds. Dad tried it and it worked! Those beautiful creatures saved my dad's life. The goat's milk coated the lining of his stomach and provided nutrients that allowed him to eat and regain his strength. He faithfully drank a glass of unpasteurized goats milk every evening for the rest of his life and ate a healthy diet.

In the 1940's few people knew of the benefits of goat milk. However, we do today. Now we are able to purchase milk along with goat cheese and many other products at a variety of grocery stores.

By sharing this story I am not suggesting all health problems will disappear if we just clink our glasses of goat milk and down the white magic every evening. What I am saying is we have come a long way. Thank goodness for chemotherapy, vaccines, and antibiotics, but we can't forget our ever-present connection with the simple healing basics nature provides us. The different worlds of medicine need to come to the table more often. To interchange ideas, work together toward the common goal of healing. Let's not waste time trying to discredit each other or let greed lead our decision making by placing profit before people.

My Dad in his WWII Army uniform

CHAPTER 7

My Personal Integrated Medical Plan

"People are very open-minded about new things,
as long as they're exactly like the old ones"
Charles Kettering

As I mentioned earlier, I was very concerned about all the drugs that were invading my body. The side effects of Chemotherapy alone would scare anyone away. Think of all the pharmaceutical commercials you watch on television. You know all the medications for diabetes, stoke, depression, the ones that list all the possible side effects, constipation, diarrhea, severe headaches, rashes, breathing problems, depression, white blood cell damage, pre-mature death! These advertisements come fast and hard on the internet, radio, TV and more. The American Medical Association (AMA) warns that the ads can be misleading to the public. Yet why so many ads? Money. According to a JAMA report between the years of 1997 when the FDA lifted many of the drug advertising restrictions and 2016 drug companies sales rose 182 percent, which resulted in a $328.6 billion revenue increase. The general public is not the only target of pharmaceutical marketing. Even Physicians are wooed by free samples, meals, drinks, and travel. Drug companies have large budgets to peddle their goods. Many individuals may be in a situation where they must take these medications for the rest of their lives believing they must live with all the side effects spending more of their hard earned money to purchase even more drugs to mask the side effects. I didn't buy into it. I wanted to find something to help deal with the known side effects of my weekly treatments, but I didn't want to ingest more drugs than I had to.

My Oncologist had given me the name of an Eastern Chinese Dr., so I followed up with her suggestion and called his office to make an appointment.

This office visit was very different from any Doctor visit I had ever experienced. Ellie and Lou both came with me. A small wind chime tinkled as we opened the door. We entered the office and were asked to take our shoes off and place them in little cubbies to the right of the door. The receptionist was friendly and had a very welcoming energy. The waiting room felt more like someone's living room than a Doctor's office. The air smelled clean. There was a comfortable couch behind a wooden coffee table of which a few books sat ready to scan. There was not one gossip magazine in site. In just a few short minutes we were all escorted down a short hallway to a treatment/examining room. No one asked me to repeat my name and date of birth. They actually looked at me as we spoke, not at a computer screen. I didn't have to stand on a cold scale so they could write down my weight or slap a blood pressure cuff on my arm.

The treatment room we entered felt like a small bedroom. On one side of the room sat a two- person couch, a chair and small end table holding a small bamboo plant. There were interesting drawings depicting acupoints (places acupuncturists insert needles) of the human body on the walls. The examining bed sat in front of shaded windows. It actually looked more like a comfortable massage table, with real sheets, not a vinyl covered mattress with stiff white paper. Next to the bed sat a cart filled with woven baskets which held what looked like clear Christmas bulbs, a few towels, and other objects I was not familiar with. There was also a small salt lamp in the room. This place was so different than a traditional Doctor office. I was used to the examining rooms filled with hard uncomfortable plastic chairs and vinyl examining mattresses covered with white disposable paper. Magazine racks stuffed with last year's gossip magazines dog eared and torn as well as a variety of testing equipment, and lighting that makes you look like something out of the Night of the Living Dead movie.

We had not been in the room very long when the Doctor and one of his acupuncturists walked in, again, very unlike the traditional 20 minute plus waiting period I was used to. The initial examination consisted of a very long conversation. His technician transcribed our conversation onto a tablet. He checked my reflexes by tapping my knee, looked at my eyes and tongue. Nothing too unusual. However he didn't just glance at my tongue as most Western Doctors do. He used my tongue to help diagnose and create a treatment. Tongue diagnosis has been used in traditional Chinese medicine for a very long time. It is believed that by looking at an individual's tongue you will have a better understanding of their overall health. When examining the tongue, practitioners look at three things: it's shape, coating, and color. When looking at the shape, if the tongue is swollen it may indicate Qi deficiency or if it's small or thin it may represent a blood deficiency. The coating of the tongue represents the health of the digestive system. You want to see a thin white coat. The color of the tongue will tell the body's internal temperature. Assessing the tongue also involves looking at specific areas of the tongue that represent the body's organ systems such as the liver, lung, spleen, heart, and kidneys because all the organs must support each other and be balanced in order to achieve complete health. I never really thought about my tongue being an indicator of my health before. He continued his examination by placing several needles into various areas of my body. Ellie was very curious as to what I was feeling and asked if he would place a needle somewhere on her. He agreed and placed one needle on the top of her head. He removed her needle and turned the lights off as the Doctor and acupuncture technician exited. I closed my eyes and just relaxed. Ellie and Lou sat there quietly, both viewing their cell phone screens. I forgot they were even in the room. After a while, the Doctor and Technician re-entered the room and removed the needles examining the areas the needles had been inserted. The Doctor then began to put together his treatment plan.

I was to go in twice a week. My treatments involved both acupuncture and cupping. He placed me on a no sugar, no gluten, no caffeine, or dairy diet. I could eat some fish like salmon. The focus was to only eat whole food, not processed. Foods that were not only anti-inflammatory but would also boost my immune system. It was advised that I eat a wide variety of foods and in an assortment of colors. He also told me to walk 40 minutes every day. I liked having a prescription of exercise and not just being told to 'move as tolerated'.

I had always wondered what it would be like to have an Acupuncture treatment. I soon had my answer. Not only did I find out, but realized I really liked it. It was so relaxing. I felt calm during my treatment and had a pleasant energy afterward unlike the artificial energy you may feel from drugs, caffeine, or processed sugar. Here in the United States many people have a hard time wrapping their heads around this type of treatment. Not only are they hesitant to have needles placed in their skin but become very skeptical when traditional Chinese terms such as qi (pronounced as "che") and Energy Channels, or Meridians (which is actually French) are thrown around. Qi can be described as an energetic 'force". It is thought of as the main force of our biological functions. "The fundamental quality of being and becoming" is how Ted Kaptchuk OMD Professor of Medicine at Harvard describes it. Meridians are like roadmaps for qi to follow or flow through to various systems and organs.

Meridians (14 in total) align with our body's systems or organs, such as gallbladders, intestines, liver, and kidneys. The Meridians sit close below the skins surface. Basically the goal behind acupuncture is to have energy freely flowing throughout your entire body. The bodily functions have been described as a river, so I imagine it this way: You are walking alongside a beautiful flowing stream where birds are singing, frogs are jumping, and all is good. Then all of a sudden you come upon a section where there has been all kinds of trash thrown into the stream. Rusted cans, plastic bottles, and old tires clog the water. The beautiful stream becomes stagnant unable to move freely. You stop and begin to pull the trash out of the stream. Slowly the water begins to return and flow freely and uninhibited. Just as you helped clear the way for the steam, acupuncture helps the flow of qi throughout your body. You go from a diseased, low energy state to a healthy, vivacious, 'take on the world' state.

Today many acupuncturists are working with physicians, Hospitals and Medical Facilities. The NFL's first acupuncturist was hired over 20 years ago. The Boston VA Hospital began to offer acupuncture to help reduce dependency on opioids and to help manage posttraumatic stress in 2013.

I was treated not only with acupuncture but with cupping as well. Yes, I received the very same treatments that Michael Phelps received during the RIO Olympics in 2016. Well, maybe not quite the same, or for the same reasons.

Cupping has also been around since ancient times. It is known that the Egyptians practiced this treatment. The basic concept is to pull blood to the skin's surface by creating a vacuum to help blood flow by dispelling stagnation and promote healing. My treatment would be called 'Fire Cupping". The technician would hold a cotton ball with forceps and light it on fire. She would place the cotton ball in and out of the cup and quickly then place the cup on my skin. It didn't hurt at all. They actually felt warm against my skin. Just as with acupuncture, I would be left alone in the room to relax. I would fall asleep. After some time passed the technician would return and remove the cups. There were times when a deep purplish circle could be seen but other times there would scarcely be anything visible. Bruising would be a result of the rupture of capillaries just under the skin.

I'm not sure how to describe the acupuncture or cupping treatments; maybe spiritual. After the acupuncturist would apply the needles or cups and close the door behind her it would be very still and soothing. My body felt calm, relaxed, and pain free.

I would close my eyes and visualize the pathways opening, the treatment helping my body clear out all the dead cancer cells, chemicals, and drugs in my system. The procedure worked. I felt stronger. I achieved my goal of not feeling any of the side effects of chemotherapy. I continued weekly acupuncture treatments and never experienced nausea, diarrhea, or vomiting, cognitive dysfunction (something they call chemo brain), depression, skin rashes, fatigue, mouth sores, or neuropathy (numbness, pain or tingling in hands or feet). I took no other medications to prevent or alleviate any of these side effects.

Let's hope the use of these ancient practices will continue to grow here in the United States, and more cancer patients will be introduced to, and have the opportunity to try these options. Hopefully, we will see more health care professionals giving them a chance before they pull out their lucrative prescription pads.

CHAPTER 8

Support is Vital

"For the positive energy spread to one
will be felt by us all, for we are connected, one and all."
-Deborah Day

Once I had a diagnosis, a treatment plan, and began to live a new normal I had to find a way to get thru it all. Many turn to organized religion or meditation. Others reach out to friends, family, the social media, or write in personal journals. The hospital offered many cancer support groups that met several times a month.

I put together my own support group. I hadn't told very many people of my diagnosis, so I didn't have many visitors while in the hospital, but a few folks found out, including my ministers who stopped in. Lou and I had become members of a church in Ann Arbor when the girls were very young. I like how our church welcomes anyone and everyone and the message is always of love and acceptance, not threats of ultimatums and hell fire. It was wonderful to see and visit with them. They helped me forget how I was feeling, as if I had just been run over by a train, hair sticking up all over and humbled by wearing a faded green hospital gown, which fit me like a large seed sack. Once I returned home, our senior minister's wife insisted on driving up with a hot meal because as she told us, "That's just what church people do!" It was delicious and I loved her visit. But as I continued with my treatments and began eating a more strict diet, I discouraged anyone from bringing meals. I decided to keep them informed but not have them share my illness with the congregation. I wanted the cancer to remain private and I stuck to my decision. A friend, who was a dietician as well as a wonderful cook, was kind enough to make a few meals for us understanding my restrictions and need for healthy anti-inflammatory ingredients, but on the whole, we muddled through on our own.

I continued to be reclusive. Maybe it was just in my genes to keep it close to home.

I informed everyone that I wanted to tell very early on. I drove up to Cadillac Michigan to tell my Mom and Sister, I had Skyped my daughter in NY, and told my very dear friend Diana. I decided to take time off from work because I worked with children and I was afraid of having a compromised immune system. I just didn't know what kind of energy I would be running on. My job involved crawling, running, skipping, or galloping up and down open non patient Hospital hallways and stairways. If I could find large enough spaces, we would do more adventurous activities such as moving on and around the large awkward Resist-a-balls. Jump ropes were great fun (as long as we kept them from tangling, becoming trip hazards or flying out of control). My boss and co-workers understood my leave although I don't believe they were too excited about taking over my active hallway fun and games. Then there was my Pilates class. This is a group of women who are intelligent, strong, and have way too much fun during class.

I had been renting space in Ann Arbor and instructing, or at least attempting to instruct, Pilates if I could ever get a word in edgewise. We call the class 'Pilates at the Plaza'. Some of these women had been in my fitness classes for years and years. Many had been with me as I taught exercise thru both my pregnancies and attended graduation open houses and anniversary parties. We watched as many of the group joyfully became grandmothers and shared tears as we lost parents. I remember sitting in our Pilates circle. (F.Y.I.; many more conversations can be carried on at the same time when sitting in a large circle). We all sat cross -legged on the floor. It was unusually quiet as I began to share the findings from the ER visit. I believe they may have been just as shocked as I had been with the news. I was their fearless leader, had been for years, barking orders in class with encouraging words like "Isn't this fun?" and "This is our happy place!" as we made our way thru the many exercises. After the depressing news was delivered, I jumped right in with instructing the class. This actually was my happy place and I truly did enjoy and look forward to the class. There was no way I would stop my teaching if I could help it. I could escape my health problems for an hour a few times a week.

It wasn't long after that class, my Pilates friends created an absolutely beautiful gift. They each individually knit a different patterned square made of soft yarn at home. Then each square was sewn together to make my very own blanket. It was amazing. I took it every Friday morning to the infusion center. It was one of the most meaningful gifts I have ever received. These are the people I chose to circle around me. These are the people who helped me laugh and forget my cancer for a few hours every week.

My mother, sister, and me during treatment

A few of my fun Pilates group members

45

CHAPTER 9

My Sanity Savers

*"The cost of sanity, in our society,
is a certain level of alienation."*
-Terence Mckenna

There was a small hot yoga studio in downtown Brighton that Ellie encouraged me to try before my diagnosis. It was in an old cool building. The windows were covered so as you entered the studio room it was dark. The old floorboards were slightly uneven, and it smelled of wood. I loved the atmosphere, and found I loved hot yoga. This was not your typical yoga class. They intermingled exercises like jumping jacks and abdominal crunches with traditional active yoga poses like warrior one, and downward dog. Class always ended with a cool scented washcloth placed gently on my forehead and the stillness of Shavasana. After my diagnosis I thought I would not be able to continue, however two of my favorite instructors shared with me that the practice of yoga along with the red heat used in the studio actually had been proven to hold benefits for cancer patients. They encouraged me to continue as long as I felt well enough to do so. So I began to take Hot Yoga classes as a way to deal with my disease. I visualized all the chemicals and dead cancer cells leaving my body via my sweat and breath. The instructors were always encouraging and shared wonderful positive messages during each session. I always looked forward to each and every class. I would feel lighter emotionally and physically as we walked outside into the cool winter air.

Along with my yoga and Pilates classes I always made it a point to get outside for a 40 minute walk every day. It helped me get thru rough days. Just being outside in the fresh air, birds singing, dogs barking, and the rhythm of my steady stride made me feel stronger.

Movement and being in touch with nature is a vital part of my being. Lou and I now live minutes from two major expressways, an elementary school, busy intersections, and strip malls, yet in our neighborhood there are many common areas. Right behind our house is a small natural area. When we moved in, we found a runoff pond and field of high grass. We have since started to plant trees and bushes in the open area although the bucks seem to enjoy rubbing their antlers on our newly planted tree trunks in the spring and the young leaves are just too tasty to pass up. I will continue to plant native plants and trees to complete my plan of a vital natural area for the animals as well as our enjoyment. Initially I worried about every deer, raccoon, frog, or crane that I saw. Where do they live? How can they find enough food? How do they get from one area to another without getting hit by a car? What kind of horrible existence must they be living with no open space to run and be free? After being diagnosed however I believe my perspective shifted. I would sit and enjoy the graceful deer walk thru, and the squirrels and chipmunks crazy antics. I even laughed as a very fat and fearless raccoon sat on my deck and drained my hummingbird feeder. At one point Lou and I gazed with amazement as a group of wild turkeys took a break sitting on our back fence, just chillin'. I walked out on our deck and took deep breaths on days the air appeared clear and smelled fresh. Gazing at the sky I sent a quiet thank-you to the universe and backyard guests.

Some of my four legged friends

Deer
mowing
the
back
yard

One of many turkeys
visiting

CHAPTER 10

My Constant Companions

"Petting, scratching, and cuddling a dog could be as soothing to the mind and heart as deep meditation and almost as good for the soul as prayer"
-Dean Koontz

As I share who my supporters were, I cannot forget to add my four legged nurses. Our two dogs Cody and Carly were there every step, bumping into each other as they ran to greet me at the door upon my return home from treatments and Dr. appointments. They would walk into my bedroom just to check on me or maybe jump on the bed if they felt a closer inspection was needed. My beautiful grey cat Katrinka was right there at the beginning also although unfortunately she passed away while I was still receiving treatments. Her health had begun to decline. She stopped eating no matter what I prepared for her, and she no longer slept by my side. I reluctantly let her move on to the Rainbow Bridge and wondered at that time if I would be joining her sooner rather than later.

I'm not the only human who values the lives of our fellow creatures. Research has shown how simply stroking the fur of a pet be it cat, dog, hamster, even cows or goats, can lower blood pressure and levels of stress. All you have to do is look around you. More and more hospitals are welcoming dogs into patients' rooms for '4 paw visits'. Schools are inviting dogs into classrooms to help calm and demonstrate love and compassion. Misunderstood pit bulls are helping to rehab prisoners, and more professionals see the value of pairing our forgotten veterans suffering from post-traumatic stress disorder with loving four legged companions. These animals offer love and companionship to humans that have taken a wrong turn, lived thru horrific experiences suffer from chronic pain or are living with disease. They create a bond that is undeniable. They are able to sense when you are overcome by depression, hopelessness, or anxiety. They are there by your side to offer licks, purrs or just a touch of a paw with no judgment. There are thousands of stories out there but one that stands out in my mind is that of Karolyn. Karolyn is an Army Veteran. After 9/11 she joined the service. Upon her return home she was faced with spine and brain injuries along with post-traumatic stress. She found herself in a dark place, living with pain, and given very little hope of relief. Her life began to change for the better after being connected with a program that provides veterans with advanced medical treatment. But she didn't stop there. She knew she needed more than the medical treatment for her physical body and found true companionship with two shelter cats named Sophia and Leonides. Coming from 2 different situations both cats had been abandoned as kittens Sophia only had three legs due to a birthing complication. The shelter had paired the two together to help with their recoveries. Karolyn took them both home and a short time later created a detachable prosthetic leg for Sophia. Karolyn went even further and wrote a children's book "Sophia the Bionic cat". This is one woman who took her bag of rocks, swung each rock into the air and hit the bull's eye with each throw. I have such great respect and admiration for Karolyn. Not only did she not stop searching for help but knew there was something more out there than just surgery and drugs to complete her healing. You can find her story at 3pawsup.com.

We live in a world where human contact continues to diminish because of social media. The human voice, eye contact, touch, let alone heart felt handwritten letters, are almost all but obsolete. We have accomplished and conquered so many human issues and problems in so many areas, yet we are losing touch with the basics of human contact and companionship. Fortunately, our relationships with our loving pets have not changed. We are still able to exchange kind words, and soft furry strokes for purring, joyful yips and snuggles. The basic foundation of these relationships are built upon unconditional love and respect. Let's revisit this basic human need and apply it to all of our relationships in our everyday life as well as in the world of healing.

Carly and Cody going for a ride

Katrinka taking inventory of Christmas

Cody and Carly warming the bed for me

Katrinka and Cody standing watch

CHAPTER 11

Finish Line
"Folks are usually about as happy as
they make their minds up to be."
-Abraham Lincoln

I cannot tell you as I came closer and closer to my last chemo-treatment how excited I was. I began looking at lesson plans for work. Rubbing my bald -head praying for my curly hair to return. I was so looking forward to no longer having my family tied down to my schedule. I felt like a little kid on Christmas Eve, all tingly and giddy. The day finally came, July 21, 2017. As Lou and Ellie flanked me, I rang the bell demonstrating the end of treatment. I was given flowers and lots of hugs and kisses. My friend Diana came over to help celebrate and we kicked the cancer can to the curb. Well we tried after numerous attempts and laughing attacks. They continued to monitor my health with regular checkups and blood draws. I also continued visiting the acupuncturist. I decided to have my port surgically removed in September. We went out to eat on my birthday. Celebrating another year of life, as well as being clear of cancer. We headed to Orlando to run the Princess 5K to top off the celebration. We came back to my wonderful ordinary boring life.

Celebrating a last treatment

Kicking it to the curb!

Ellie and I after the
Half Marathon

The gang with Minnie Mouse
after the 5K

CHAPTER 12
PART II

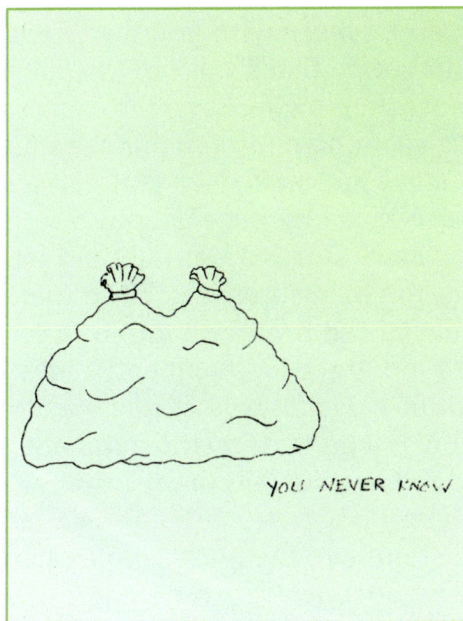

YOU NEVER KNOW

You Never Know

"We all have to go through the tumbler a few times
before we can emerge as a crystal."
-Elizabeth Kubler Ross

This was supposed to be my last chapter and as I sit at the computer today my head is spinning. I had it all figured out I would tell you how my family and I had traveled to Orlando, Florida, and completed the Disney 5K Princess run to celebrate my beating Ovarian Cancer; That I had returned to my normal life, although realizing now, Cancer will always be in my rear view mirror and I will never really return

57

to a true normal. Once diagnosed there will always be the follow up Doctor appointments and tests, not to mention the insurance statements which arrive monthly, that continue to remind you of your pre-existing condition; All constant reminders that the cancer could return at any time. Yes, I had hoped to share with you my last checkup was a happy one. However, that's not how it played out. I had fallen off the horse somewhere and the cancer had returned. My CA125 was again high (although not as high as the first time) and my CT-Scan showed several masses on my brain among other areas of interest thru out my torso. Yes, the ovarian cancer had returned not only in just the expected abdominal area but in my brain also. The chances of ovarian cancer traveling to the brain are found in less than 5% of patients. Lucky me. It was September 27, my 62nd Birthday, when my Saint of a daughter Ellie had spent her afternoon off from work driving me to the hospital and then sat with me as I waited to have the MRI of my brain.

We sat there listening to the noise coming from the waiting room television no one was watching. We watched as children and adults paraded through stopping at the desk pulling out insurance cards and signing forms at the request of an expressionless receptionist. Ellie pulled out her phone and we watched a few funny gifs for a little comic relief. I dutifully drank the two cups of chalky fluid that had been flavored with a sickly sweet flavoring which the not –so-happy nurse brought out to me. I felt sorry for everyone, including Ellie, and me, who had to sit in that ominous room.

They called my name I changed into the faded hospital gown 10 times too big and entered the room I had wished to never see again. After walking by a metal detector I lay back onto the little bed. The technicians stuffed earplugs into my ears, and to prevent any movement placed soft pads around my head. I rode the track into the little tunnel as the loud machine noisily took pictures of my brain. I closed my eyes and tried to think happy thoughts, like I was just on a roller coaster as it clanked up its rail preparing for a drop. But no fun drop ever came. We had no sooner arrived home, finished our dinner and enjoyed a piece of Birthday cake with the dogs, when I received a phone call from the Oncologists office. They had received the report from the MRI and wanted me to pack a bag and drive to the emergency room to be admitted into the hospital that evening. I freaked out. I pictured the character Johnny from the movie 'The Shining' with his crazed eyes and stringy hair sticking his head thru the smashed door calling "Here's Johnny!" This was the making of my very own horror film! It couldn't be happening! I was going to be the poster child with no more episodes for the rest of my life. We had registered to run the Disney ½ marathon this time in February 2019. Cancer couldn't possibly be back so soon! The Universe however saw it differently. As I packed a few overnight things I couldn't help but think about the wonderful vacation Lou and I took just a few weeks prior to my oncology checkup appointment. We had gone to the lake shore of Michigan. Our friends Laura and John offered us a few nights at their cabin at Crystal Mountain Resort. If you have never visited this area you really should. It's amazing. We had hiked two major sand dunes to Lake Michigan and back. One had been so steep we were laughing as we climbed back up on our hands and knees. With each movement up we sank into the warm soft sand. We had rented bikes and rode to a nearby town ate a delicious lunch and jumped on our bikes for the ride back. I remember jogging along winding side roads in the mornings, passing beautiful tall trees, smelling the scent of pine and autumn, which was fast approaching under a clear blue sky. I felt so good, invigorated, and alive.

How did I do all this with three tumors on my brain? I will never know the answer. But I do know that our bodies are amazing and mine was strong.

After we arrived in the ER Ellie texted the numbers 911 to Lou's cell phone. Part of a code I later learned the two had decided upon should this very thing happen. He was in Grand Rapids at the time and although he assured me he had not gone over the speed limit he must have traveled with the Jedi's at the speed of light to arrive at the hospital before they had even moved me from the ER into a hospital room.

As expected, a battery of tests were ordered, IV's hooked up and multiple white coats walked thru my door. My nightmare had returned. Don't get me wrong: if it were not for these incredible people I would not be sitting here typing away, listening to Cody snore by my side, thankful for whatever extra time I have been given again. I just didn't think about or want to be reliving it again.

As tests returned, we found ourselves speaking to surgeons, radiologists, and Oncologists. Looking back I can only believe the powers that be must have thought I had the condensed Readers Digest version of cancer the first time around and I needed the full text experience, because I was about to experience a whole new world of treatments and Doctors. I sat listening to the plan, and thought to myself, am I ready do to this all over again? Aside from a lingering headache I felt so good, I just couldn't believe the cancer had returned and returned with such a vengeance in my brain.

I refocused. Our first step was to deal with the three tumors on my brain, so let me start with my surgeon. He was the new guy in the practice. Now this could mean he is seeing me because he needs to fill his schedule, or he just graduated and lacks experience, or he had been practicing for a while, but left another practice for an unknown reason. Just who was he, and how many brain surgeries like mine had he actually done? I am sure as he had walked down the long, busy hallway to my hospital room he had many questions about me. Such as how I would react to the news he was about to deliver. He entered the room and introduced himself to Lou and me. He had a very calming demeanor and was very thorough in giving us in laymen terms, just what we were dealing with. I actually had three tumors. He shared what he felt was the best plan to follow, along with possible options. There were several possible serious side effects with this type of surgery due to the location of the tumors. One of the possible negative side effects was face recognition. Lou's biggest fear was that I would awake, look at him, and ask the question "Who the heck are you?" There could be possible coordination, balance, and vision as well as speech problems. Some may or may not be temporary. Very scary news, but after much discussion we all decided on surgery. Two of the tumors were too large to be treated with radiation alone. He would remove the first on Monday and, if things went well, he would remove the second four days later on Friday. The third tumor was smaller and would be treated with radiation. He left the room. Lou and I just looked at each other. Could this really be happening? Was I really going to have not just one but two brain surgeries in one week?

No stopping now. Everyone had a heads up on my low pulse and blood pressure and the anesthesiologist made up a cocktail that worked for me. I have to tell you this: the surgeon was all that. After I was scheduled in the ER all the nurses and support staff continued to tell me what a wonderful surgeon he was and how lucky the hospital was to have him. Not only did he get rave reviews of his abilities as a surgeon but as a human being. That, I could clearly see, and it moved him to the top of my rating chart, as well as give me more confidence in his abilities. As they moved me into the surgery prep area the following Monday, I tried to stay positive.

They began to wheel me into the surgery room. Zero hour. I was ready. Bring it on! I kept visualizing the tumor removed-gone, Asti La Vista Baby!

The first surgery was three and a half hours. I awoke to people scurrying around. I was still very groggy. I heard Lou's voice and focused on his face. I knew him! That brought a big smile from both of us. We quickly moved into the first healing phase.

I continued to pass the tests: following fingers as they moved from right to left of my face; touching someone's finger in front of my face then touching my nose. Waking up to a light flashing into my eyes several times a night (initially every hour). I was asked to resist as my hands and then my feet were pushed against.

I did so well with the first surgery and was recovering so quickly that the surgeon moved my second surgery up from Friday to Wednesday. This time the second tumor was removed on the other side of my brain. My mantra this time was 'There is no place like home." If I had red slippers, I would have clicked them together. However because I had no shiny red shoes-only size XXXL tan hospital socks that kept sliding off my feet-no clicking was involved.

During the recovery from the second surgery I found myself trying to get comfortable with a turban of sorts wrapped around my head to protect the incisions. It felt like a stiff papier Mache crown. I threw myself into recovery mode again. Lou and I walked the halls and even went downstairs and out the front doors to walk the hospital property which, I'm sure was against the hospital rules, so we didn't ask. Lou has always said just do it: you can always ask for forgiveness later. I just had to get out and into the fresh air. When Ellie joined us, we took another walk down to the hospital gift shop. She bought a lavender shower bomb to place in my shower when I was cleared for a shower and wash my hair, which I was so anxious to do. It wasn't long before I got the shower okay. I used the shower bomb and it smelled heavenly. Even the nurses commented on how wonderful my room smelled. I can only imagine the smells the poor nurses walk into. Little things like getting fresh air, and the lavender scent, lifted my spirits, and gave me momentum. A Physical therapist and Occupational therapist (both very young with no sense of humor) visited me. I felt sorry for these young professionals as they stood in my room. They were just doing a job- entering and exiting hospital rooms listed on their clipboard- following protocol. If only they took time to actually hold a conversation with the patients. Share human stories and show a little interest. Something that can't be taught and something you see so little of these days. I passed all of the physical and all but one mental test. It was a type of story problem. I panicked as I had a sudden flashback of being in elementary school and the teacher calling on me to answer a question in front of the entire class. I hated those horrible story problems! I answered the question incorrectly. After they had gone out of my room, I kicked myself for being so stupid. I felt confident that after a few more days had passed, I was able to get more than an hour or two of solid sleep and ate a few good meals brought from home everything would be functioning just fine.

All I could think about was going home. The nurses were having a hard time keeping me contained in the small room. I believe they were actually just as anxious to hand me my discharge papers, as I was to receive them. Early one morning the surgery team entered my room after I had just taken a shower. I was dressed in street clothes ready for another morning walk. The senior Physician scanned the small room and made a comment that the patient must be in the bathroom. The Nurse Practitioner said, "No that's her right there." I reached out to shake his hand with a smile. After we had a short discussion, my discharge orders were written. I immediately rolled up my yoga mat and gathered my birthday and Get Well cards that had been placed around the room.   I grabbed my cell phone from the tiny table that swings over the bed knocking everything else off and pushed the home button. The minute Lou answered I said (quite possibly yelled) "Get here as soon as you can! I have my papers they're' letting me out!"

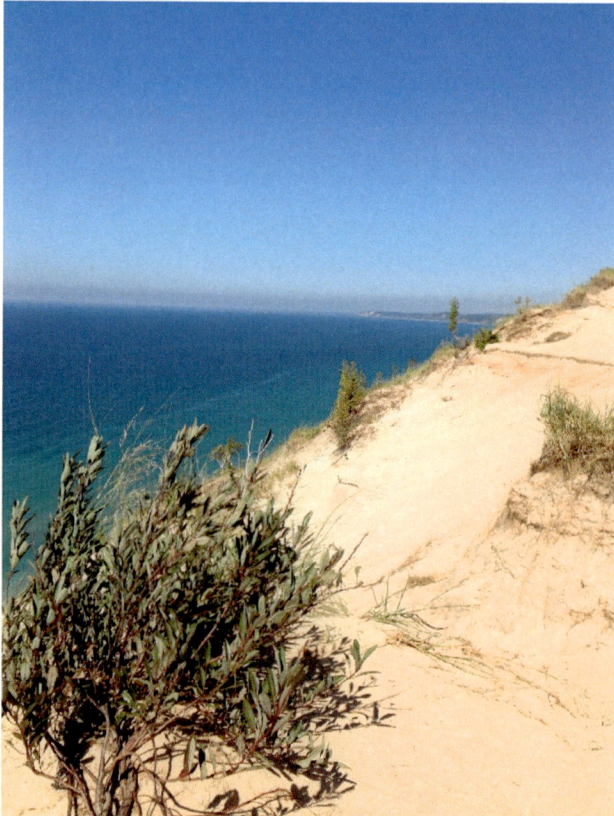

Sand dunes on beautiful Lake Michigan

CHAPTER 13

THE NEXT BATTLE

The Next Battle

"Beam me up Scotty"
Captain James T. Kirk

The next plan of attack was Radiation. I was to receive radiation thru what they call 'Cyber Knife". Which is a very precise beam of radiation pointed directly in the area needed. In my case, the brain. Having chemotherapy drugs slowly dripping into a vein attacking cancer cells as well as healthy cells was frightening, but radiation took my fear to another level.   I was told I must lay perfectly still on a table as a type of futuristic gun moved around my head sending rays of radiation thru my skull into my brain attacking any remaining cancer cells from the large tumors which had

65

been physically removed and zeroing in on the third tumor. My very first visit left me very nervous and anxious. The area was under renovation; there was plastic hanging from the ceiling, ladders and such sitting around, as well as makeshift rooms. The staff appeared disoriented and maybe a little frustrated. The intake nurse appeared distracted and rushed. I was in line for another CT Scan as well as the creation of a facemask. The CT scan was a piece of cake. I knew what to expect and breezed thru. This scan was to be used as a type of road map for the Doctor to use to send the rays into the precise areas of the brain to attack the cancer cells.

Creating a mask was very interesting. They placed a warm mesh like material over my face. I had to close my eyes and wait until it cooled and stiffened before they would lift it off. While the mask was hardening two thoughts entered my mind: one, if this is what it felt like when they made Michael's creepy mask in the movie Halloween and two, if my skin would feel smooth and wrinkle free once the mask was lifted. Probably. And it didn't. I returned the next week for my first actual treatment. Lou and I voiced our concerns and my anxiety level, so we were greeted with answers and a better description of what was going to happen during the 5 treatments.

I would first meet with a nurse who would take my vitals and weight then be taken into the treatment room. We walked into a white room. The walls, I was told, were very thick and filled with lead. No homey feel here. There were very large pieces of machinery attached to the walls with tracks that ran across the ceiling. One looked like a futuristic gun from a star wars movie that hung ominously over the bed. I climbed onto the adjustable bed, which could be raised and lowered thru a remote control inside as well as outside of the room. As I lay down, they placed a cushion under my knees and a very thick and wide rubber band around my feet. I held on to a soft ring with my elbows relaxed by my sides. The mask was put on last and attached to the bed. All of this is done so that my body and head would remain perfectly still and in perfect alignment during my treatment. My mind began to wander. I drifted back to my childhood and watching The Sir Graves Ghastly T. V. Show which aired a variety of monster and horror movies. Most of the movies had horrible acting and the visual effects had much to be desired but for kids with wild imaginations it was wonderful. I remember one such movie where the doctor had gone mad in a sterile white room much like the one where I now lay.

My journey down memory lane was suddenly interrupted when the technicians told me they were escaping, I mean, exiting the room. There was a short period of time when the technicians came in and out of the room making several adjustments some I barely felt. Then they came over the intercom and announced the treatment was about to begin. They had put on a CD playing Elvis Presley music. I began to hear a loud clicking and see a smooth movement of the gun like machine around my head. Strangely enough I did not feel panicky or confined and fortunately I never felt the urge to itch or sneeze. I visualized this super machine zapping all the microscopic cancer cells that may have been left behind from the two surgery areas as well as blasting the living daylights out of the last smaller tumor. I then exhaled their remains out of my body. Actually any dead cancer cells are eliminated thru the lymphatic system, but I needed a better visual. The time passed relatively quickly and then it was over. The first of five visits complete. I had two more treatments, then the weekend off. Lou and I headed up to Cadillac for a quick family visit.

When my sister and her husband came over for dinner Saturday night, I discovered my brother -in -law actually worked on positioning the space age radiation equipment.

He shared how thick the walls were to prevent any radiation leakage and how they used laser beams to place the huge equipment into the room. There could be no room for error especially with the Cyber Knife. What a small world.

Monday and Tuesday the following week I wrapped up the radiation treatments. After my last visit I could hardly wait for my discharge papers and to walk out the door. I was asked if I wanted my facemask, so I took it. Not sure what I was thinking. It could be recycled into a bird feeder or a table centerpiece for Thanksgiving but, then on second thought, maybe not. It was actually unceremoniously buried in the back yard.

The weeks following radiation passed relatively uneventfully. However, as time went on, I felt more fatigue and nausea, which never really went away. My taste buds and sense of smell went haywire also. I would think I was really hungry for something yet when I actually had it in front of me my taste buds seemed to have left the building.

As far as my sense of smell, everything seemed to be in hyper mode. My husband loves his Lysol spray, so when he is making the bed, vacuuming the carpet, or emptying out garbage pails, he goes berserk with the spray. Well, this disinfecting style just had to end. The smell, for some reason, just pushed me over the cliff. I would run out of the room covering my face. He shelved the spray at least when I was around.

My final visit with radiation seemed to take forever to arrive. I was very nervous that the last tumor had not been destroyed. I received wonderful news. My Doctor was very happy with the results of the last MRI. The smaller of the tumors had actually shrunk and the areas in which the two larger tumors had been were looking good as well. In fact she called me an over achiever.

I didn't want to think about the fact that radiation continues to be in the body long after the treatments end. It can remain months even years killing cancer as well as healthy cells. I wouldn't let this overshadow the fact that the radiation had accomplished today what it was sent in to do and I was ready to move on to the next round of attack. Chemotherapy. I had to first have a new port implanted as I had foolishly removed my first. The following weeks brought nausea and hair loss which is something I had hoped would not occur until after at least a few of the chemotherapy sessions.

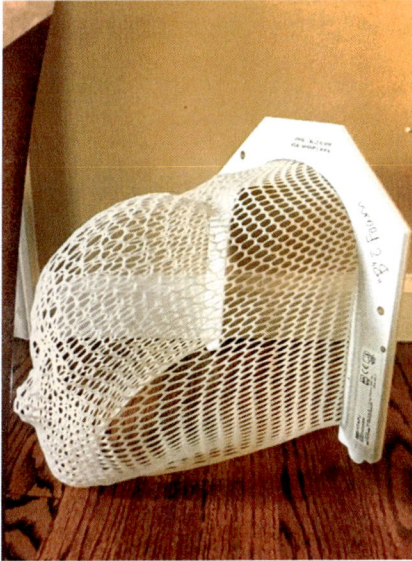

My lovely radiation mask

Sir Graves Ghastly 1967

CHAPTER 14

FRIENDS

Friends

"Friendship is the only cement that will
ever hold the world together"
-Woodrow T. Wilson

Many friends had reached out to me this second round. I welcomed all the cards, texts, plants, and flowers that came my way a little easier this time. Not sure why. Maybe the first diagnosis came to me as such a shock I needed the time to deal with it myself. It was as if I was in an alien land and needed to gain my bearings. I believe I was embarrassed. I believed it showed signs of being weak. How could I admit I had cancer? I was the strong healthy one, the Instructor that had run a marathon in Hawaii. I had taught 2 or 3 fitness classes sometimes more every day for years. I took very little time off during or after my pregnancies. This time around I didn't feel as guarded. I had kind of a "what the heck" attitude. I had another round to go, this time with brain surgery, radiation, and chemotherapy. I knew I would be shutting out the world again, refocusing on what is important which so easily slips away in our everyday lives. Our Country is in turmoil right now. I was still unhappy with what was going on in our Country, in Washington. The terrible attacks on people, our environment, and threats to our freedoms. I kept asking myself, 'where have all the Hippies gone?' It's like we are at a big rock festival, not the fun kind where you sit on a green lawn having a picnic listening to live music, but one from your nightmares, where people have gone berserk, madder than heck throwing rocks at everyone and everything. I miss the peace sit-ins and free hugs. Hippies were into communes where everyone living together worked things out, grew their own organic food and shared and recycled possessions.

People seem so agitated these days, so unwilling to compromise, so sure it's someone else's fault that they are in the situation they are in when actually they are responsible; no one else collected their bag of rocks. It appears we have become a society not looking for ways to solve our problems, but that of pointing the finger and jamming the courts with lawsuits that no one really benefits from except the lawyers' overseas bank accounts. Our phones and screens are full of graphic pictures and reports relaying worldwide violent crime scenes in real time, not to mention reality and talk shows where people are yelling at loved ones not willing to see each other's point of view. How did we get here? In the 1970's I was a psychology major in college, and I remember reading the many studies on the effects of violence upon the human brain. Some studies reported children's cartoons were too violent: That Bugs Bunny was too mean to Elmer

Fudd, the Road Runner and Coyote were too violent when they flattened each other, then popped back up at amazing speed and started the chase all over again. At the time I thought, I wasn't a violent person and I had enjoyed watching those very cartoons, but maybe those studies were warning us of what was ahead. Maybe it was the beginning of our world's acceptance, even fascination with violence, and we didn't listen. Looking back into my young adult years people flashed 2 fingers, the universal sign for peace and used words like "cool man", today people yell 'F-you!" and flash the middle finger, demonstrating the same offensive message. Kids today actually play games where they mutilate, even kill, people after personalizing them. The media exploits the privacy of parents who have just lost a child to gun violence, or individuals who have lost all their worldly possessions to climate change by plastering their heart wrenching interviews on every screen across America. Holding onto our sanity is getting harder and harder these days. When life tragedies overturn our world, or disease grabs hold of our physical body, we begin to look for emotional support. Many don't know where to turn.

According to the Center for Disease Control more teenagers die of suicide than cancer, heart disease, HIV, birth defects, stroke, pneumonia, influenza, and chronic lung disease combined! The numbers of children who are exposed to gun violence and suffer from emotional and physical side effects are on the rise.

No wonder part of the intake process for cancer patients are questions based on mental status. "Do you have thoughts of suicide, or harming yourself?" Receiving news of having cancer alone is enough to make one feel helpless. Many families today are spread across the country which alienates the family unit. Add on what's happening in the world today and there is more than enough to push us all over the edge.

You have to pull yourself out of that sinkhole to find what is good in your life and reach out.

The comedian Red Skelton once said. "Live by this credo: have a little laugh at life and look around you for happiness instead of sadness." I decided to do just that and reached out to my circle. I had friends come over for coffee. Lou and I went out to dinner with couples we had not seen for a long time.

After my second radiation treatment, I traveled over a couple of buildings on the hospital campus to meet my friends and co-workers. It was great to see them. Although we had kept in touch thru texts, feeling their hugs and seeing their smiles was wonderful. We were truly a happy team who tried to help families live healthier and happier lives. We believed and lived our philosophy. We sat around the worktable and caught up with each other's lives.

A group text was born made up of my sister, Katie, Ellie our good friend Diana, and of course myself. We have great fun sharing everyday happenings with wit and humor. The daily group text keeps us all up to date and always brings smiles and chuckles.

My sister suggested I read a book "The Persian Pickle club". It is about a group of women in 1930 that form a quilting group and their friendship. It is during an especially stressful rainless summer and the hardships this group of women and their families' shared. They had next to nothing, but they had each other. They were like any other group of women, not always agreeing, or understanding each another's actions, but they gave everyone room to be themselves, and didn't judge. When one experienced one of life's hard blows the rest of the group rallied, taking turns visiting, searching their kitchens for ingredients to make a homemade meal to drop off, or search their small stash of fabrics for a quilt piece to share. It made me stop and think, there are days I may feel my bag is too heavy, but people all around me have heavy rocks of their own to carry. We need someone in our corner at times, but then we also need to be there for others. And that's really what it's all about, isn't it? I should just stop my bellyaching.

I enjoyed reading the book. It took me out of my situation and back in time when every-day life may have been physically harder, but less complicated. Human contact and conversation was special, there wasn't the constant barrage of ringing cell phones, blaring T.V messages or computer emails from unknown and often unwanted solicitors.

I was enjoying the freedom of catching up on reading, visiting with friends, driving up to visit my Mom and such between treatments so I decided after this second reoccurrence to retire from the Hospital. Although I only worked part time, it was more a full time job. Every 10 weeks the participants were different. Each session brought families with different physical abilities as well as a variety of ages and motivation levels. I spent many hours looking for and creating activities to customize the workouts outside of our weekly meetings. A perky social worker at the hospital suggested that I apply for Social Security- after all I was 63. She was fun to talk to and helped us with all the paperwork. Funny thing, I make as much now through Social Security as I was making part time at the hospital. Retirement already. I always thought I would work into my 70's but I guess that's what cancer does, puts a rush on things. I knew as I wrote my resignation letter, good or bad, this was the end to a big part of my life.

CHAPTER 15

ONE LONG DARK WINTER

"Nobody trips over mountains.
It is the small pebble that causes you to stumble.
Pass all the pebbles in your path
and you will find you have crossed the mountain."
-*Author Unknown*

We were fast approaching three very busy, sometimes hectic, and for some people, stressful months. November is when we take time to be grateful and enjoy a delicious meal with family and friends, followed by December with the celebration of lights and Christmas, and of course January when we say goodbye to the old and welcome in the New Year, full of hope and expectations.

I was feeling pretty confident and very thankful. Two brain surgeries within 3 days, five Cyber Knife Radiation treatments completed, and I was ready to take on the chemotherapy portion of my treatment, or so I thought. Unpleasant side effects followed the radiation. I became very nauseated and tired. However, I had no idea just how miserable I was about to feel in the coming month.

Chemotherapy was next.

The plan was one Chemotherapy Infusion every three weeks for a total of eight infusions. I'd been down this road before. I knew one of the pre meds given would be Benadryl which would put me to sleep minutes after it entered my blood stream thru the port, so I pulled out the only thing I knew I would need, my Pilates blanket, threw it into my bag and climbed into the car with Lou and headed to my first infusion. The major drugs used would be Paclitaxel, Carboplatin, and Dexamethasone Sodium Phosphate, along with all the premeds and fluids to hopefully prevent nausea, or any allergic reactions. Because of the potency of these chemotherapy drugs my Doctor feared I would not be able to create enough blood cells between infusions, so I returned to the cancer center to receive an injection 24 hours following the treatments to prevent my white blood cell count from dropping below the acceptable level. Many possible side effects of my infusions were the same as before, nausea and fatigue being the most common. How bad could it be as I had already experienced these after my radiation treatments. This time around however, they hit me like a brick wall. Food didn't sound, look, or smell good, let alone taste like anything.

When I did eat anything it tasted like cardboard and it sat in my digestive system like a rock. I lost weight. The health staff told me to eat anything that would go down, even junk food. My friend who had battled cancer several times told me I had better eat, or they could admit me into the hospital should I continue to lose weight. What? Just how scary is that? It was a huge effort, but I sure as heck did not want to go back into the hospital. So, please pass that cardboard! The other side effect I felt was lack of energy. My "get up and go had got up and gone!" Although I had felt my energy was drained a bit prior to chemo I had never felt like this before in my life. When we were young, there were times when my Mom used to send my sister and I outside to play due to our enthusiastic "rough housing it" as our Mom would call it. Later as I became a fitness instructor, I had been called the energizer bunny, and even taught a fitness class the night before I delivered Katie. So to be so tired that it took an all-out effort to simply lift myself out of a chair was extremely foreign to my entire being. I felt horrible.

One afternoon I had taken a short walk with Carly around the block thinking the cold fresh air would revive me like it has so many times before. However as I entered the house, I was so exhausted that I plopped down just inside the door boots and all. I told Carly to grab her own good dog treat. Of course she couldn't and gave me a dirty look as she trotted over to sit by the fire. This was not to be the worst of it. Our family was about to be hit with an unexpected emotional blow. Our wonderful golden retriever Cody was diagnosed with cancer. I was completely dumbfounded. It happened so fast. He started to be selective on his walks, only going once a day and would tell me when he was ready to return home. I thought he was getting older and was just reminding me he was in charge. I of course obeyed his requests. Then he stopped eating. I called his vet right away as Cody loved his meals and snacks and I knew something was wrong when he turned down all opportunities to eat. I was able to get an appointment right away. So on November 30th I put him in the car, and we headed out. The Vet ran a few tests. He returned using terminology I was way too familiar with, Hemangiosarcoma (tumor of the vascular endothelial cells), and enlarged lymph nodes. He told me that we would have to make a decision of surgery within hours, as it didn't look as if he would make it thru the night if we didn't. How could this be happening? The bad news just kept coming! Phone calls were made, and our family of course voted surgery. Lou came home and we drove Cody to the Animal Emergency Center. Everyone had a sleepless night, as Cody had never spent the night away from us let alone in a veterinary hospital. He came thru with flying colors. The entire staff fell in love with him of course. Who wouldn't? He was such a wonderful dog.

We had him home in a day. Things were going very well and although they sent him home with one of those horrible cones to wear around his neck so he wouldn't lick his stitches- you know the ones that drive the dog crazy- he never had to wear it. Lou put a T-shirt on him thinking that might be more comfortable and fulfill the same job. He managed to take the t-shirt off all by himself and never licked the stitches once. He was such a smart dog. I was so happy to have him home to take long naps with me, to sit by my chair as I attempted to eat breakfast and greet me at the door whenever I returned home. We took short walks and he even took a few car rides. We made a plan that the two of us were going to beat cancer together. Cody returned to his vet and had his stitches removed December 7th. Everything was looking good. Maybe our luck had changed.

The winter dragged on. I still wasn't getting the relief I needed from nausea and fatigue. I felt like a tiny hamster, not getting anywhere on her little exercise wheel. I was taking drugs with side effects of nausea then anti-nausea meds to try to mask the side effects. I returned to my thoughts of integrated medicine. I was already eating healthy, and exercising, so I decided to apply for a Medical MJ card. After the November 2018 election in Michigan, Medical Marijuana had become legal. I had been told that this wonder plant, among other talents, had helped relieve the symptoms of nausea for many cancer patients. So I began the grueling task of filling out my portion of the paperwork. I handed the next portion to the Oncology staff to fill out and obtain my Oncologist's signature. I wrote the check and handed over the envelope to my local Post Office to deliver to Lansing, our Capital, which is just a short hop, skip and jump from our home. We watched our checking account, anxiously waiting for them to cash the check, knowing after that deed was done it would simply be a short time after I would have the card in my hand and we would be traveling to a nearby dispensary and my symptoms would soon be history. Wrong! They cashed the check but returned the paperwork in its entirety as the Doctor's office had neglected to fill out two short lines. I had to start all over again at square one by picking up an entirely new application package of forms, getting them filled out by the appropriate people and return everything with the addition of an extra page explaining this was attempt number two. Something that sounded so simple and should have been quick turned into a project that took months.

The whole card experience was just frustrating but when Cody suddenly took a turn for the worst it was devastating. We thought we were well on the road to enjoy Cody's sweet company for a few more years but it just wasn't to be. His health quickly declined, and we lost him on December 28th, a short time after his joyful return home. It was as if he came back to us just to say goodbye. I was more than sad; I was completely beaten down. I felt totally alone and missed him terribly. I cried every day. Everywhere I looked I missed his presence. His big brown eyes and soft furry coat. How was I going to get thru my treatments without him? For a while I didn't think I would, between feeling ill from my treatments and not having him by my side I simply didn't think I had the energy or even the desire. The two of us were going to work thru our cancer, together, sharing our bad days and good days. But he was gone, and I was left to battle on. Time passed slowly. I eventually could talk about Cody: how he loved to play in the snow, lean against me, and join us in the pool for a swim, without crying. The pain was still there, and I knew it always would be. Cody, Katrinka, Andy and all my past beloved pets are forever in my heart. I had to face the fact every day the sun was going to rise, and I had to get thru the day fighting cancer without Katrinka and now Cody by my side.

I continued to feel nauseated and awaited my Marijuana card. Then it hit me. Why wasn't I searching for another acupuncturist? I began to search for one with training and experience in our area. A good friend passed on the name of an acupuncturist in Ann Arbor. Not only did he fill my requirements but came from a long family line of acupuncturists. I called his office (well actually Lou called) and grilled him on his education, philosophy, and if he had worked with cancer patients. He passed the Lou interrogation. Needless to say I made an appointment as soon as I could. After meeting him I felt comfortable right away. I liked his style and confidence. He answered all my questions patiently and because I had had some experience with acupuncture, I knew a little more walking in. As I entered his office there was a large chair and slightly larger couch both cozy to sit on. A large desk sat in front of the sitting arrangement with a beautiful bamboo plant. The hallway was to the left of the desk and it led to eight treatment rooms each filled with a soft twin size bed and a cart holding needles and such for the sessions. Half the rooms had windows letting in sunshine should the weather allow. He had lovely calming artwork on his walls and played soothing music. After the very first session I began to feel relief; my symptoms melted away. I began going two times a week. As acupuncture had worked when I had my first round of chemotherapy, I felt more energy. My nausea disappeared, and my appetite began to return. I eventually did receive my official Medical Marijuana card in the mail but by then acupuncture had once again eliminated all the side effects. My family was disappointed that I didn't at least meet with a counselor at one of the many cannabis dispensaries. I believe they were secretly thinking it would be fun to have their Mom using weed. January continued to be dark and cold. I missed my dear Katrinka and Cody. I found some nights feeling very low and just plain tired, but the next morning I would wake up feeling more energized and thankful I had another day. I looked for little goals to work towards. Some days it would be just getting thru the day. Other goals were much more grand- like running the Disney Princess half marathon in February. Before the reoccurrence of my cancer we had registered for the half marathon in Orlando as a celebration of being cancer free and darn it all, I was going to complete that run. It may not be a celebration as originally planned but I was still alive, wasn't I? I glued sequins to my big puffy blue taffeta skirt and running top, purchased tights to match as well as 'Bomba' Socks. I walked on the treadmill daily, continued to teach Pilates and followed my favorite Hot Yoga Instructor to her new Studio. Carly continued to lead me on daily walks. My Oncologist was a little worried to say the least. She suggested we cancel the treatment just prior to our leaving for Florida but I didn't want to drag out the treatments any further into spring, so I kept my appointment at the infusion center. During that infusion, my favorite nurse and I talked about the half marathon and how much fun it was going to be. It just so happened that she, her Mom (who happened to be my nurse navigator) and I had many things in common, one being the fact that we were all running the same half marathon. I was not concerned that I would pass out or fall. My goal was to finish the route before the little blue bubbles swept me up into their van. These bubble people may sound innocent; after all we are talking Disney the land of enchantment. However the bubbles quietly follow behind the runners who are lagging behind and should they not make the cut off time for the race they are swept up and put in the white bubble van. No one wants to cross the finish line in the back of a van.

As I had hoped we had an awesome time. It was a beautiful race day morning. We were surrounded by fun colorful costumes and jovial runners. We watched with excitement as fireworks splattered against the dark morning sky as each section of runners before us was set loose. Soon it was our turn. It didn't take long after our fireworks went off and our coral began to move forward, that my daughter Ellie left me in the dust. I saw the look in her eyes, as we began, she felt the need for speed; I knew that feeling so I sent her on her way with my blessings. I jogged a bit and walked a bit. I had kind of an interval thing going on for a while and I felt good. I took advantage of every water stop slowing my pace down to get in line to grab a cup of water. After a few miles I knew if I was to finish, I had to shift from an interval pace to a fast walk.

 I told myself to keep the pace nice and steady, stay hydrated and enjoy the whole experience. I felt as though I was the slow moving but determined tortoise in the story of the Tortoise and the Hare. Nothing was going to stop me. I kind of liked the idea of being a turtle. Turtles represent persistence and longevity; something I hoped was in my future. At about mile 10 I heard someone calling my name from behind. It was my infusion nurse and her mom my Nurse Navigator. Although they had started before me, and were faster than I, they had stopped to enjoy the many Disney distractions along the route. They must have sighted my huge sparkly blue taffeta skirt. I was so happy to see them. They slowed to my pace bless their hearts, and after a few more short miles we swiftly walked together under the Finisher's Arch made entirely of colorful balloons to collect our medals. Lou was right there to cheer us on. He had been tracking my cell phone all along. Unable to cross the fence to get to me he climbed up and balanced on a trashcan to reach over and hug me, that is, until a security guard yelled for him to get down. I did it! Cancer did not stop me from being me and accomplishing my goal! My family enjoyed a few more carefree, beautiful days in Orlando, before we returned to the cold and hard reality of my treatments.

In March things were humming right along; acupuncture, blood draws, Dr. appointments, and counting the weeks until my last transfusion, when I acquired a small red rash. They believed it to be a reaction to the Carboplatin, one of the chemo drugs. So as a result, I would need a De-Sensitization treatment. This was then added to my long schedule. The added treatment involved administering the drug causing the reaction at a slower rate under more observation, so, oh yes, it took basically all day. Lou took me to these appointments I slept, and he brought his laptop from work.

The last week of March couldn't arrive fast enough because that signaled my last infusion and de-sensitization appointments. A good friend was visiting, and he videoed me ringing the bell. Again. We ran out to the parking lot. Oh happy day! I fully enjoyed the moment- sending out texts and making phone calls happily relaying the message that my treatments were again over. One month later during a follow up appointment I was told I had a small blood clot by my port. I was told this was not unusual and my clot was very small however I should go on a blood thinner ASAP and probably would be on one for the rest of my life. Not exactly what I wanted to hear. My Oncologists started me on a shot, which I gave myself every morning in the abdominal area. My midsection soon took on a yellowish brown color due to all the bruising. After much pleading and two Doctors later I was able to stop the shots and go on Xarelto which is a tiny chicklet size pill taken once every evening. Initially I kept confusing the name with a flea and tick treatment for dogs, which brought puzzled looks from family and friends, but I finally got the drug name correct.

Our precious Cody Dog

Lou illegally reaching over the fence

The second bell ringing

CHAPTER 16

How My Support Engine Worked

"It's about the TEAM, the TEAM, the TEAM
-Bo Schembechler U of M Coach

My name is Lou better known as Marie's husband. We have been together for more than 30 years. We met in a fitness class. I was the annoying one. In the end I won her over. After raising two strong and confident daughters we are entering our next chapter in life. At the end of 2017, we threw ourselves a party to celebrate those 30 years and danced the night away. Little did we know that in a few short months our lives would change so drastically.

In the ER that night, we heard the diagnosis and that next chapter had a new definition. To say we were shocked is an understatement. Our family had been healthy our entire lives. But ovarian cancer...seriously? After a few minutes I pulled myself together. Marie already told you I was a health care executive and had worked in hospitals, physicians, insurance companies and medical centers to develop and improve health care programs and services. Well that knowledge and experience was about to become tested.

When I looked up, I saw that Marie was in shock. Through my tears I told her "WE GOT THIS!" I asked to read the test results, asked a few questions- what did this mean or what did that mean, what is our next step. The doctor referred us to a specialist. I asked if we could speak to them at that time (it was 11:oo p.m.). She called the oncologist. While waiting I Googled the specialist, read her background, and learned she worked with non-traditional practitioners. The next google search was to find non-traditional practitioners in the area. Boom found one. Shortly thereafter we were talking to the Gyn-Oncology nurse manager. She explained what the next few days would be like and asked when we could meet. We set up that first discussion for Saturday in our hometown. We thanked everyone, Marie got dressed, and we walked out holding hands... paying the ER $250.00 co-pay.

Reality set in. Marie's role was to get better...disease free. My role was to be her husband, advocate and create a team. I became Captain Lou. The core of the team was me, Ellie, Katie, and Marie. We set short-term goals, based on the principle "put first things first." We needed a plan of action and overriding principles to operate.

Goal 1. Tell her you love her! Tell her often and show her in many ways. Laugh, cry, talk.... be normal.

Goal 2. Communicate effectively and often. Tell Katie what was happening. Agree on how best to communicate and how often.

Goal 3. Learn all we can about ovarian cancer. Research, read, meet with experts to identify what may lie ahead. That included NIH research, Ovarian Cancer Research Foundation, physician associates, best practice, outcomes, survivors, insurance coverage, drug coverage and more.

Goal 4. Secure the right resources at the right time. Seek out recommendations, review best practices, and meet providers to get a feel if they could fit on the team.

Goal 5. Create a schedule and timeline. Identify who, what, where, how and when.

<u>Goal 6.</u> Review the plan and revise as needed.

The following Wednesday, a port was inserted. Our journey had begun. TEAM Candiotti was formed and ready to go.

My first "to do list" before the first face- to- face meeting with the specialist included the following:

1.   Determine if the specialist was the right one? What was the education background, where was the fellowship completed and when, what articles was she author or co-author, was she active in research, how was she recognized professionally and more. This would give me a sense of who she was, how she thought and whom she worked with.

2.   Was the proposed treatment plan the best one for this type of cancer? What was best practice and outcomes? It's different by region of the country and what health care system is involved.

3.   Was the hospital system state of the art? What resources would we need, what type of research was taking place.

4.   What did the insurance plan cover, what common codes were used, what was the co-pay and deductible? Where were the pitfalls? What experimental procedures or practices were included or not? How to compare your explanation of benefits with your hospital bill.

5.   What did the prescription drug plan cover and not cover? Brand name versus generic, medical marijuana or other herbs, what am I responsible for and compare it with your written benefit plan description. Sometimes the payment denial is wrong.

6.   What were common problems associated with each of the above. Don't assume providers talk to each other. Always obtain a copy of a report or record and carry it with you. Confirm appointments made. Make sure the right facility code is being used,

7.   Identify what Team Candiotti needed from the providers, insurance companies and each other. Who were the right persons to contact and how best to contact them. Who is in charge? What we needed was honesty, transparency, and information. No sugar coating just the facts as we know them.

8.   Identify what the first week would look like. Then the second week and so on. Who would be involved, their roles and more.

The first meeting was with the Nurse Navigator. She provided the important information regarding procedures, ports, and treatment plan. I asked what we could do to help Marie feel better physically as her swollen belly had not gone down but gotten worse. Cell numbers were exchanged, a calendar was developed, schedules synced, and a procedure scheduled for Monday to drain her abdomen, then a port inserted.

So much information was learned. The right resources were identified and secured. The timeline was created. The team was communicating. Don't forget.... it's about Marie, not the cancer.

I realized that to get through this I needed to be the project manager. I would bring my professional experience to the table, identify a system and process, and manage it to "get er done!" This provided us all structure to organize our thinking, develop a plan, communicate the plan, identify, and invite resources to participate and keep our focus. The vision was to have Marie become disease free. The execution of the plan came next.

As the Team Captain I would always ask myself the following:

1. Did you tell her you loved her today (morning, noon, and night)?

2. What is our goal today? Do we have the right person at the right time (driver, treatment buddy, nurse, specialist)?

3. How will this make Marie feel? What side effects should we look for? What can we do first to alleviate those side effects? When do we call you?

4. How can I assist you (physician, nurse, insurance company, pharmacist) so that you can give your best effort possible?

5. Is this the best solution or action today? What are we missing? What did we forget?

Trying very hard not to lose our minds we created what every team does:

Team Name: TEAM CANDIOTTI

Team Members: Marie. Then Captain Lou, Ellie, Katie, Marie's Mom, Doris, Marie's Denise and Floyd (Marie's sister and husband), family friend Diana; the oncologist, the nurse practitioner, the Chemo nursing team. We extended team membership to others as we needed them. The TEAM kept growing.

Team Color: Purple

Project Goal: Disease free!

Team Mantra: *Kicking it to the curb!*

I also need to remember, this is about Marie, my love. Don't forget that. We are not defined by this cancer. We are defined by the love we have for each other and our family. Many more people were about to see just what that meant.

That first Friday, her first day of chemo was a whirlwind. So much information on drugs, medications to alleviate side effects, what to expect 1,2,3 days after treatment. So many notes taken. My keen observation skills and 5 senses were on high alert as the chemo started to enter her system. They stayed on high alert for the many months to come. Within seconds she had a reaction. "Marie, what are you feeling?" She responds, "I have a warm sensation..." as her face turns fire red. The nurse immediately stopped the drip. Turns out she was having a reaction to the drugs. What do we do. Wait it out. Be patient, let's see if it dissipates. If not, we will start Benadryl then the chemo again. Seriously you want me to be patient? That is something that doesn't come easy to me.

Now we have information to create the day-to-day medical treatment, medication monitoring, nutrition, acupuncture, rest, check-in (so not to disturb rest), exercise, and more schedule. We have information regarding nutrition, how to monitor and treat side effects, when to build in exercise, rest periods (naps) and more. I had to chuckle about the napping. I remember the advice we had when we had children. When the baby naps you nap. It applied now...when Marie naps, you nap.

A new routine developed, which helped us gain our sanity back and not let this take us do now. Believe in Marie, our daughter Ellie, the professionals, treatment, and healing that would be taking place. Now back to our daily ritual.

1. *Goal 1.* Being able to love someone and show that love took on new meaning. It is being about in the moment. Ellie and the smoothie, hold her hand, listen and just being there. Assure her each day is a win and that tomorrow will add to our win. I needed to slow my roll and focus on the most important person in my life.
2. *Goal 2.* Checking in with each other throughout the day. Marie and Ellie, the schedule, Candiotti provider resource directory, the notebook categorizing everything (thank you Ellie), calling to say hello, I love you and more. Staying organized, having a process and system helped reduce my fears and be in the moment with Marie. We leaned on Ellie's organization skills to create the system.
3. *Goal 3.* Look, listen, and feel. Those keen observation skills came forward and were an asset throughout the journey. This was tested when the side effects started to hit. Chinese acupuncture can treat these. Let's get scheduled. And so it came to be, acupuncture 3 times per week every week to alleviate side effects. Or, finding an alternative to painful daily blood thinning stomach injections. Oh, hematology, let's call. Yes, there is an oral medication that can replace it and be just as effective. It made Marie feel better.
4. *Goal 4.* Assisting providers. The most important thing was to make sure the providers were communicating, reading, listening, and responding to each other. Are notes entered into the medical record regularly, yes. But are other providers aware something new happened, not necessarily. So we call and let them know. Leave a message with the nurse navigator. Some responded to email. Some call you

back. Some give you time in the hall. This should sound familiar, as it describes a normal workday, doesn't it. Exhibit those leadership skills. Being clear is kind, be concise, be compassionate. Listen and help steer if necessary. Be thankful for their time and expertise. Even when you want to sometimes shake their marbles loose.

5. *Goal 5.* The best solution. Challenging the facts, the protocol, the policy, the feedback, the plan, answer, and more. It comes from a place of love and commitment to provide the best for Marie. Nothing more. "I'm sorry, you can't go back there, it's for patients only." Well, thank you for sharing, however Marie is pretty darn scared right now because she doesn't know what the next hour will look and feel like. Can you tell her, us? Maybe we could walk back there to show us both and that can help. Could you please make that happen? We would so appreciate this. Thank you so much! Yup, wanted to shake this person's marbles loose.

Captain Lou was fully engaged, as was TEAM CANDIOTTI. One day at a time, one success at a time, one problem at a time. It keeps from getting overwhelmed. Here are a few examples:

1. A drug treatment required contact with a specialty drug company. I call our insurance company to make sure it's covered. I call the drug company to make sure forms are completed and signed so that they and I can talk to each other about Marie. I call the local pharmacy to let them know the specialty drug will be delivered and please text me when it arrives.
2. The insurance company doesn't authorize a standard of radiation treatment for a brain tumor. The hospital calls to tell me this 1-hour before we leave the house. That's ok, I say, I can sign the waiver

92

accepting responsibility for the treatment cost. I know I can contact the insurance company liaison assigned to my employer to handle the issue on the back end. The hospital was surprised that I wanted to keep the procedure time and that we would be leaving shortly. I sent a quick email to the insurance rep. and we were on our way. When we arrived, the service line director agreed not to charge us, the physician had put a call to the insurance company medical director, and I had emailed the liaison. The procedure took place, and halfway through I learned the insurance company approved the treatment.

3. Treatment alternatives. Painful blood thinner shots were necessary following chemotherapy. That's the protocol. Yet, it became unbearable for Marie. Let's pursue alternatives. The ovarian cancer specialist is only familiar with that medication. OK call the primary care physician who refers us to a hematologist, who prescribes an oral blood thinner. I worked in health care. But I can navigate the system. Was it more complicated than that, yes. But you get the idea. Get er done!

4. Outrageous bill. It was bound to happen. All at once, physician office visit, lab draw, hospital treatment bills all came at once. It didn't make sense that they were denied by the insurance company. I called the insurance company who simple needed to know that Marie didn't have any other insurance plan that would cover her medical services. It didn't matter, that their own files would answer that question. I needed to attest to it. Then I called each provider to let them know what transpired and to re-submit the claim. Get er done.

There were days it drove me crazy. The TEAM was there to talk me down. There were days full of worry. The TEAM let me share. There were days I needed a break. The TEAM filled in. The TEAM, the village, the support group, the cancer community, the church ladies...call it what you want. You can't get through it alone. TEAM CANDIOTTI is alive and well! It always was. We had the foundation to beat this. Marie will lead the way. Marie will kick it to the curb! The TEAM will be behind her all the way. *The TEAM, TEAM, TEAM!*

CHAPTER 17

Happy Planet – Happy Life

A Nation that destroys its soil destroys itself.
Forests are the lungs of our land,
Purifying the air and
giving fresh strength to our people.
-Franklin D. Roosevelt

With the return of my cancer and loss of Cody to cancer, the question of just where this disease came from began to haunt me. So many healthy people and happy pets with no family history of cancer have been, and are being, blindsided with a cancer diagnosis every day. Cancer is a creepy dark entity dancing all around us. It's ever closing in presence touching all of our lives. The first person in my life who was diagnosed with cancer was my great Aunt Ida when I was still young and in school. She went into surgery for a routine procedure, they discovered cancer throughout her body, stitched her up and sent her home to get her affairs in order. She was in her 80's. I lost a brother-in-law to Hodgkin's. He was only 21. My first husband died at 33 from complications of bone cancer. He had been told his symptoms were just stress. Just a few years ago a fellow fitness instructor was diagnosed with cancer. She was in her 50's. Fortunately, she beat the odds and continues to instruct fitness classes at a ridiculous time in the morning before she goes to her real job. I lost another friend to ovarian cancer in 2019. Yes, we both had been diagnosed with the same cancer and both dealt with the disease at the same time. She was a fellow fitness and swim instructor; an incredible person and I think of her often. I lost yet another good friend and member of our Pilates group. She had breast cancer that had metastasized. Her loss was a huge blow to our small group as she was an energetic powerhouse, and an incredible friend to us all. Why? Today we have a wealth of so called expert advice at our fingertips. Countless health magazines splatter their cover pages with 'How to Beat Cancer', "How to live a healthy lifestyle" or 'How to live a Cancer Free Life'. After typing in 'Cancer' your computer search engine will pull up multiple sites giving you helpful advice on how to avoid cancer, and what to do if a loved one has cancer. The program I had taught fitness for at the hospital was created to teach families how to live healthier lives and avoid disease but clearly there is no guarantee.

Even with all the knowledge we have, we seem to be losing our grip, if we ever really had one in the first place. It appears to be a modern day version of the Plague. They are unable to tell you how or why you have it, and there still is no cure. Although Motown's Marvin Gaye was singing about social injustice the lyrics from his song "What's Going On" is so fitting here. We continue to look for a cure. Research is ongoing and research money continues to pour in. New cancer treatment centers are opening up across the Country; hospitals are investing billions of dollars in building new cancer wings and Infusion centers. More cancer specialists are appearing claiming to give you more years of survival if you switch to their practice. Pharmaceutical companies are making millions on those of us with the disease. Truth is Cancer is big money. I understand that if it weren't for the research and todays Doctors, I probably would not be writing this book, and I'm thankful. But after all these decades there still are no answers as to why or where our cancer came from.

So what gives? Why is cancer, along with so many other diseases, on the rise not decline? I, along with millions of others, believe it is all around us, the toxic environment we live in, due to the decades of constant chemical attacks we have been launching on our skies, water, land, and us.

There can be no doubt that the human species is absorbing these very chemicals that billion dollar companies are dumping. This is humankind's war on the Garden of Eden, a war on us. Nothing like trashing God's creation. We are unable to continue the abuse of our planet with such viciousness without harmful effects upon every single creature and plant that exists upon Mother Earth. We knowingly release into our air, seep into our water, and saturate our land with known carcinogenic chemicals. The damage is extensive, but I also believe if we stop dumping the disease causing chemicals, we all could be living healthier lives and our future generations will have the chance to do the same. I believe the answer is just that simple. Maybe we should not only be researching a cure but researching just as hard for its origin. As Apollo13's Jack Swigert's famous statement exclaims: "Houston, we've had a Problem".

In 1997 Sandra Steinbraber Ph.D., wrote a book, "Living Downstream". Sandra holds a doctorate in biology from the University of Michigan has authored and coauthored many publications on ecology. A cancer survivor herself she voiced her scientific based concern for our environment and our health 20 years ago. She continues to do so through her many publications and public appearances.

So why have we not pursued the health of our planet and ourselves? A problem man has struggled with since the beginning of civilization: Greed. Multibillion dollar Companies whose huge profits depend upon pollution dumping practices. They have the money to pay off local inspectors and Government Officials and have for decades. Companies claim small amounts of these cancer causing toxins released daily will not harm us, yet it doesn't take a PhD to see daily exposure to these toxins turn into weeks, weeks turn into months, months turn into years and years turn into decades. Decades of toxic build up in a contained planet and in our bodies. Just as disease deteriorates a perfectly healthy body, these toxins are deteriorating our perfectly balanced eco system. We know they have been dumping for decades with larger and stronger amounts of chemicals as each year passes. So, just as prayer is no match for gun violence, wishful thinking will not make our toxic living conditions disappear. These companies have big profit goals and will never develop a conscious. They need to be held accountable for their actions and should no longer be allowed to hide behind their self-funded studies, false claims, and payoffs.

Fred Bahnson is the director of the Food and Ecology Well Being Program at Wake Forest University School of Divinity, I believe he summed it all up when he said, "We've had an ongoing infatuation with heaven that has caused us to ignore the Earth and to desecrate the actual places in which we live." We are so busy making our lives easier and more comfortable; we don't even realize what we are doing to the very planet that gives us life."

This planet we live on is not just a beautiful playground. Our entire existence relies upon it. So why don't we take care of this paradise that was given to us?

When Lou and I were first married we lived in a cute little cape cod in the city of Ypsilanti. A few years passed and we began thinking of moving to a larger home as our family was growing. We had begun our family with a bossy cat then expanded our human family members, bringing home two beautiful baby girls. Space was becoming sparse. It wasn't long before we made yet another addition to our family. Lou mentioned one summer evening he knew of an older couple who were moving to Florida and couldn't take their dog with them. I felt sorry for them but really didn't think too much of their dilemma until this very couple pulled into our driveway with their four-legged child. Of course I knew once

Katie and Ellie laid eyes on the beautiful red retriever a family vote of any kind would not be needed. He jumped out of the van and everyone ran around the little yard squealing and barking with joy. Before long and without looking back this red beauty leaped over the two steps onto our porch and through the front door into his new home with his new family. Andy Dog had no transition period. It was as if he had lived with us from the start, and we absolutely fell in love with him from the moment we saw him.

So with the recent expansion of our family, we decided to start looking for a larger home with a little more gusto. We hit the jackpot, finding an acre lot in a nice neighborhood in the Township of Saline. We had a nice big yard for the girls and Andy to play and built a red brick home large enough for us to knock around in. Neighbors were great and we liked the schools. We were living the American dream. We spent a lot of time out in our yard. Lou loved and still does enjoy landscaping. He has quite a green thumb and turned our yard into a beautiful garden. As you drove through our new neighborhood one of the first things you noticed was the lush green yards. The problem was, as in many American neighborhoods, the healthy lush yard is a façade. Most families hire companies to treat their yards with deadly chemicals to keep the appearance of healthy grass. We forget the whole purpose of our yards is to simply prevent erosion. Today anything that deviates from an acceptable blade of grass is viewed as public enemy number one. The dandelion is such a plant. Not only is it a pretty yellow flower, for generations people actually ate the plant which provided then, as it does now, many vitamins and health benefits. We are told no decent homeowner should have such a plant in his or her yard, so we remove it, usually with poison. Are you aware that the lawn service business of today began after WWII ended? Companies that had produced toxic chemical and biological weapons for the military had to find someone else to sell their killer product to. They did, unsuspecting Americans across our country. Marketing was relentless, and still is. This product that we by choice are spraying on our trees, bushes, and grass to keep up with the Jones's may just be killing us. 53% of most pesticide products that are applied to our lawns include possible carcinogens. 'Possible carcinogens' have been defined by the International Agency for Research on Cancer (IARC) as well as the United States Environmental Protection Agency (USEPA). 32 of the killing pesticides cause threats to insects such as bees, ladybugs, butterflies. Fact check: These insects that we are killing are vital to our own food chain. It also kills more than 70 million birds every year. It pollutes our vital water supply along with killing many aquatic organisms. The USEPA also reports 60 million pounds of synthetic pesticides are used each year in private yards and gardens. Even more are used in public spaces like city parks and schoolyards.

The problem is not only in America. 41% of these pesticides have been banned or at least restricted in other countries. Many families have no idea just how lethal this practice is and what they are exposing their families to. Several years after we moved our family to Saline, we were using a yard treatment along with everyone else in our neighborhood. One summer we began to notice all our beautiful trees we had planted over the years were dying for no reason. These trees mind you were not little seedlings. They were trees that were almost 20 years old providing much needed shade and shelter for not only our enjoyment but also home for local wildlife. After Lou did some digging around, he found our yards had been treated with the pesticide Imprelis. There was a group lawsuit against the chemical company, of which we became a part. We had to provide before and after pictures of our yard as well as fill out an endless amount of paperwork. The lawsuit covered only trees, not any other parts of our beautiful lawn that was destroyed. Following the disaster there was the usual diversion of finger pointing deflecting from the real issue at hand.

The fact was our neighborhood, as well as many others, had been poisoned. If this pesticide was lethal enough to take down 10-15 foot trees, what about us? Every household in our subdivision had well water. I believe this killer pesticide found its way into the water we ingested and bathed in every day. We spent time out in our yards with our kids and pets. We unknowingly absorbed these toxins and carried them into our homes. I believe this pesticide played a part in my cancer diagnosis. The huge chemical company had assured us that all other living things were safe but how could that be? It was created to kill and kill it did. Unfortunately, as in many of these group lawsuits, after the complaints stopped and the checks written the problem was soon swept under the rug. The pesticide was relabeled and put back on the market

Maybe we should use a basic guideline from now on; never ever trust, let alone, purchase anything that is created to kill because what goes around comes around. We can stop this poisoning simply by not using a toxic lawn service, and demand our public land such as schoolyards, playing fields and parks not be sprayed. It has not been done because these companies lobby hard in Washington. The overreaching companies continue to put profit before our health and well-being.

My family was exposed to another known carcinogenic after the kids had grown, and long after Andy had moved on over the rainbow bridge. We downsized and moved north a bit to the city of Brighton. It wasn't very long after the move into our new community that big oil began fracking about 25 miles from our new home. Just the description of fracking should make the little hairs on the back of your neck stand on end. Drilling into the earth with a high-pressure water mixture of sand, brine, toxic metals, radioactivity, and hydraulic fracturing fluid, not to mention miscellaneous chemicals that the oil companies do not have to disclose to the public. According to Breast Cancer Action over 700 chemicals are commonly used. Many such chemicals are listed as chemicals of concern because they are known carcinogens. No one is able to determine where or how far these chemicals travel once underground. A simple experiment of spilling a cup of water on the dinner table or spilling a cup of coffee in a car will tell you there is no way of controlling where the liquid will go, the same is true for fracking. I believe these carcinogens entered our home via our well water and also played a part in my cancer diagnosis. America is able to stop this unhealthy practice by making fracking illegal and going green. Should be simple. However the oil companies are allowed to continue this harmful practice and put big profit for the 1% before the general population.

These chemical attacks are not our only worry. The exposure to air pollution, including methane and carbon dioxide has been continuous since the development and expansion of the industrial revolution in the 1780's. Levels are advancing rapidly and appear to be out of control today. Today's administration continues to roll back restrictions on these toxic chemicals creating greenhouse effects harming us all and bringing huge profits for the super-rich.

When my folks first built their home in 1951 there was nothing but cornfields, woods, and open spaces around the area. At the time it seemed to be a perfect spot, walking distance from town, but far enough from town to enjoy a little peace and quiet. It took just a few years before 'progress' began to move in and the houses became surrounded by an interstate highway, complete with a front door view of entry and exit ramps.

Fast forward to the 1960's when my cousin and I would play for hours in the cornfield that sat behind our row of homes much to the farmer's disapproval as we at times would leave our homemade tents made of old sheets and rugs as well as discarded kitchen pots and pans behind in his field for the next day's play. We also rode our bikes up and down our little street playing wagon train. When stopping to water our make believe horses (our bikes) we discovered the car dealership that had been built at the end of the road was discarding their soapy water from the car wash, old oil, and gasoline gunk into the stream through a long pipe.

Clearly, they knew they were polluting this little stream we played in as they had installed the pipe. They chose to save a few bucks by dumping instead of legally disposing of these chemicals. As they continued to allow this gunk to pour into the little stream, my cousin and I would remind them every so often of their illegal actions by stuffing various vegetation into the pipes to slow, and on occasion even stop, the black gunk from flowing. As children we know what is right from wrong, but as we age, we forget what is really important and greed and materialism overshadow our thoughts and actions. Air quality in the area was steadily diminishing. There were fewer trees and green spaces around us to absorb the noise and pollution. The traffic noise and the car exhaust became intense at times during the summer months, but because we had no air conditioning and depended on a breeze to cool our home, we kept our windows open. Installing an air conditioner was considered a luxury not a necessity in those years. It's unheard of today to build a house without air conditioning. With today's climate change and the extreme heat we are experiencing I cannot imagine not having it. Sadly, many of our poor and ill here and around the world have to suffer without relief.
My little story happened 50 years ago, today we continue to destroy our physical and mental health in the name of progress and convenience.

Our air quality continues to be a growing problem. According to NASA for centuries the atmospheric carbon dioxide was never at or past the 300th cut-off line. 2018 recorded the 400th line. What does this mean? All we really need to know is it is fast approaching dangerous levels and rising roughly 10 times faster than the average rate of the ice age recovery warming. When our air quality is low humans suffer from headaches, insomnia, and nausea, not to mention respiratory complications and disease. It has taken no time for the pharmaceutical companies to find pills, and inhalers, to mask the symptoms of all these conditions. According to a 2018 study published in "Nature," humans are not alone in negative side effects. Our plants suffer and produce less nutritious fruits and vegetables. With poor air quality this will lead to future nutritional deficiencies around the world. Our planet suffers with higher temperatures and higher sea levels, making our existing coasts disappear. Humans are moving inland causing even more overcrowding which is a health issue alone. It is clear all forms of life suffer. The problem is widespread. There are many sources of carbon dioxide, but one of the biggest offenders I'm sure you are aware is car exhaust. Because we don't actually see it, and unless you spend time outside to smell the odor, it is hard to visualize just how much carbon dioxide surrounds us, so maybe this will help. Think back to one of your visits to a Natural History Museum. If you were lucky, they had a huge replica of a 9-ton T-Rex on display. Now imagine each and every Ford Expedition sold spitting out enough toxins into our atmosphere to fill an entire T-Rex dinosaur every year. This is just one vehicle. Now imagine the toxins we expel every rush hour every day. But wait, it gets worse. When the Trump administration took over, Ford lobbied to repeal vehicle emission standards to save money. Don't fall for those pretty pink ribbons they stick on the back of their trucks. They have no business pretending to fight for cancer survivors like me.

The car industry is doing even more than their share of contributing to the cancer epidemic. Being a Michigander, I know how important this industry is to our state. I believe we have the know-how and the ability to make more than fancy cup holders and flashy dashboards. For the first time in decades we could truly be world leaders and cut all emissions.

All of these actions are now affecting our entire planet's climate. In just the short 62 years I have walked this sacred earth, storms and weather patterns have changed dramatically, and to say the earth has sped up heating on her own is ridiculous. Mother Nature has always had her own timetable it's called slow and easy. Just ask any forester, scientist, or geologist.

In 2019 we experienced temperatures way below 0 during the month of February followed by more cold, snow, and ice/rain mixes though the months of March and April. If one more person says, "Well that's Michigan!" I'm going to burst. My memory may be fading, and I certainly remember some things more than others, however, this is not the Michigan weather of my past. We actually had seasons, spring, summer, fall and winter. Storms were minimal. I actually played barefoot in puddles after a thunderstorm and looked for rainbows. I had no fear of floating away from a flood caused by a sudden torrential down pour, or a wind shear appearing from nowhere violently yanking up huge healthy trees, or hail plummeting down the size of baseballs. In the winter we had snow days where school would be closed due to a large snowfall. We would spend all day playing outside in the white fluffy stuff, sledding, making snow people and forts under blue skies. Today we have too many school closings due to ice storms and severe cold, not snow. Our kids are denied having fun outside on their inclement days off.

Our storms aren't just storms - they are storms on steroids. Growing up I can remember only one major tornado that swept thru my hometown in the spring of 1962. I was 6 years old. Everyone talked about that one storm for years. Today we don't even have a chance to clean up the destruction from one storm before another storm strikes.

So let me ask another question. If our air, water, and land are polluted, how can our food possibly be safe to eat? I have counted the many recalls made on the food we purchase from our trusted grocery stores. There are too many self -driven studies with companies' self-interests at stake, so many underlying issues, undisclosed information and so few answers given to the public. One of the most recent cases hitting our courts in the spring of 2019 involved Glyphosate a chemical found in Monsanto's weed Killer Roundup used by most of our large food growing companies. Quaker Oats is just one of many breakfast cereals found to have considerable levels of this cancer causing chemical, yet their marketing continues to target individuals with heart conditions, and children. The pesticide Chlorpyrifos is also still on the market. There is evidence that this chemical may harm developing brains of our children. Outbreaks of E.coli make their ugly rounds, disappearing just long enough for us to forget then reappear with nothing being done to prevent this killer. Labeling our food is a huge battle and is ongoing. If these food companies have only our best interests in mind, why won't they print their sources and contents on their labels? In March 2015 Representative Mike Pompeo (R-KS) re-introduced the Safe and Accurate Food Labeling Act. Sounds like he had your best interest in mind, right? Wrong. This bill would deny Americans their basic right to know. It would prevent the FDA from mandating labeling, and it leaves all labeling up to the food companies themselves. We already know they are not transparent and only come clean when caught and unfortunately that only happens when we the consumers become ill, or worst, die from their toxic, unsanitary practices!

What can we do?   After many sleepless nights and much fingernail biting, I came to this conclusion. We must all make our own decisions as to what we eat, with what information we have. I consume everything in moderation. Food that is grown on small organic farms near our home is the best I can do. I buy organic, not to prevent disease, because I already have cancer, but because it is the right thing to do for my kids and my planet. I pay attention to each and every dollar I spend, because as they say, money talks. On occasion, should I eat flesh, I make sure the animal has actually walked in a yard or field and felt the warmth of a sunny day, not lived in a windowless box in its own bodily excretions. By being more conscious of where I purchase food from and the amount I purchase, I am also able to control the amount of plastic wrapping that enters my home, and eventually the landfill.

With the creation of plastic man created one of the most harmful materials to our world. When plastic came on the market, we all thought what an incredible discovery! We welcomed it with open arms: No more bottles that could break, easier food storage, plastic bags with fancy logos at every store to carry our purchases home in. Automobile companies put it in cars and trucks and the list goes on and on. In fact it's hard to purchase anything these days that is not made up of or packaged in toxic plastic.   Our fish and animals are killed daily by ingesting plastic, believing it is a food source, or becoming so bound in the discarded waste they are unable to free themselves.

Plastic simply does not break down, it lasts forever. It takes 450 years for one plastic bottle not to disintegrate, but to break down into pieces. Plastic is in our rivers, lakes, and oceans, in our forests, fields and roadsides and in our very own bodies. Research has been ongoing, and we now have proof humans are ingesting plastics. In one such study scientists found up to 7 different micro plastics inside healthy human digestive tracks. Philipp Scwabi, co-author of the study, stated "Now that we have the first evidence for micro plastics inside humans, we need further research to understand what this means for human health."

We knowingly as well as unknowingly come into contact with hundreds of cancer causing chemicals every single day, and because all living things are intertwined, we are being re-exposed over and over. I feel we are all playing a game of Russian roulette hoping our genes are strong enough to battle the toxic environment we have created. We must come to grips with this fact and nurture all of nature's binding relationships, not poison them. We are able to do just that through caring and respect for all of nature and for our fellow man.

Ellie and our first golden, Andy

'My gang' enjoying a beautiful summer day (I'm the one on the far right.)

My dad and our kid wagon train, 1959

CHAPTER 18

Lessons To Be Learned

"People are not going to care about animal conservation
unless they think that animals are worthwhile."
-David Attenborough

Here in Michigan we experienced an extreme cold spell with temperatures well below 0 in 2019. The piercing cold made me feel like staying under the covers. I crawled out from under the warm blankets grumbling about the cold trying to find my slippers, which have been again shoved under the bed. I headed into the kitchen to make the coffee and prepare breakfast. As I looked out my kitchen window, I couldn't help but smile at the birds (chipmunks and squirrels I must add) busy eating seeds from the feeder, sipping water from the heated bird bath, singing, and looking absolutely beautiful. The squirrels and chipmunks looked fluffy and spunky. They were chasing each other, flipping their tails, and taking turns trying to climb the bird feeder pole only to slide back down or execute perfect back flips onto the ground. They see another day of life- another day of flying with their flock or scurrying with their family. They awake each morning to live fearlessly.

The animals spend each moment by simply living, unlike their human counterparts who approach each day with a list of things to conquer, egos to be feed, and missing the whole point of this beautiful life. We have always studied and observed their behavior not as fellow earthlings but as superior beings. Those who study and work with animals know how very intelligent they are, and we have much to learn from their world, and also that maybe we are not all that superior. For decades we have been aware that the animal world self-medicates. The science of self-medication is called Zoopharmacognosy. Anyone who has owned a cat or dog will know that they eat grass to help eliminate hairballs or parasites. A pregnant elephant in Kenya will travel miles to find a particular tree only to give birth shortly after. Following their childbirth they become devoted and loving mothers. Women in Kenya actually mimic this by creating a drink from the leaves and bark of this tree to help them go into labor. Orangutans in Indonesia will search and locate a particular plant, chew the leaves to create lather. Then spit the leaves and lather out to apply it as humans would apply a topical salve. Nearby villagers grind these leaves to make a balm for sore muscles.

Amazingly there are lizards that will eat the root of a certain plant if bitten by a venomous snake to combat the poisonous venom that has been placed in their system. Researchers in Uganda have observed chimpanzees in the wild eating the bark of the Albizia tree for gastrointestinal problems. The disappearing female monarch butterfly, if infected by a parasite, will lay her eggs on a plant that is fatal to the intruder.

Ira Pastor, the CEO of Bioquark, Inc, in Philadelphia states, *"We live with other organisms which from a health and wellness perspective are much further advanced than humans. No other species tries to cure with any single solution. Nature employs multiple options. We're not appropriately imitating nature yet."* Brenda Morgan Ph.D. states, "Nature and humankind are inextricably bound to one another. They have a living, co-creative relationship, and a union of the life force, which can catalyze the evolution of humankind. Humans and nature must come to rest with each other, must unite." I am excited to see all the work that is being done in this area. I am also distraught over the fact we are still destroying miles of habitat around the world possibly destroying the very plant or plants that could possibly cure all forms of cancer as well as other diseases. A perfect example is the Yew tree. In the early 1980's researchers discovered Taxol or Paclitaxel a very effective anti-cancer drug, from the Yew tree. It was part of my chemotherapy treatment both times. The Yew tree almost became extinct here in the states because of this, until they were able to use a newly discovered method of pulling out the needed substance from just the leaf and not destroy the entire tree. China has stepped up to the plate to meet the worldwide demand and has planted 2 million trees to this date and plan on planting another 5 million in the near future. We must pay attention and look at our past to preserve our very future. I found this story in the book: "The Meaning of Trees" by Fred Hageneder, *"The story of Gilgamesh was the most popular and widespread tale throughout the ancient Near East. It relates how a man named Gilgamesh visits a cedar forest in a quest for timber and, falling prey to his own greed and desire for fame and eternal life, destroys the forest and its spirit guardian, the giant Humbab. But the consequences are dire, for he finds himself also responsible for the death of his dear companion, Enkidu, and in bitterness and despair loses his own life as well as his afterlife. The ecological moral in this legend is obvious, and interestingly, it is the oldest written text humankind possesses. Fragments of this text have survived in Sumerian, Akkadian, Hittite and Hurrian, indicating its wide distribution."* We need to listen.

I know we are capable of revitalizing nature, and every so often you hear of just that. Being a true Michigander, I love the Great Lakes. In the 1960's they used to call Lake Erie the dead lake due to the heavy industry that lined its shores. Waste from city sewers, fertilizer, and pesticides from agricultural run off all added to the lakes pollution. Vacationing on Lake Erie was unheard of. Fishermen used to say there were times of the year if the water splashed on their skin it would actually cause a burning sensation. It all came to a head after the Cuyahoga River, which flows into Lake Erie caught on fire. In 1972 the U.S. and Canada signed the Great Lakes Water Quality Agreement to lower amounts of pollutants entering the Lake. In that same year Congress passed the clear water act in an attempt to tighten regulations on industrial dumping. Although we need to do much more to bring this Great Lake back, we are on our way. The fishing has slowly been improving, and the mayflies have returned. Mayflies are wispy flying insects that only live for 3 days. These harmless insects had disappeared for decades due to the pollution but are now making a strong comeback. This is proof that we can work together and do great things for the environment.

Let's put our human egos and drive for wealth aside, admit our existence and health depends upon clean air, water, and soil, as well as the health of every plant, and creature on this planet, from the mighty bumblebee to the loving elephant. We must respect all life forms, not destroy them. Our very future depends upon it.

CHAPTER 19

SO NOW WHAT?

"Each golden sunrise ushers in new opportunities
for those who retain faith in themselves,
and keep their chins up. No one has ever seen a cock crow
with its head down. Meet the sunrise with confidence."
-*Alonzo Newton Benn*

Some people say all things happen for a reason. I'm not convinced. And I don't think we are 'selected' to have certain experiences during our short walk on this planet. Why do some people live charmed lives and others endure a hard and miserable existence? No one knows. When tough experiences are thrown our way and our bag of rocks get heavier, we must make a decision to either trudge on or give up. Maybe that bag of rocks Uncle Pete was talking about wasn't just about decisions we make in our lives, but how we all experience life. Not about holding on to every rock we collect but about what to let go. Maybe it's about what rocks we choose to keep, and what rocks we learn from and send back to the universe.

From the moment I was diagnosed to today, everything about me has changed: physically and mentally. During treatment, the taste of toothpaste changed. I had to change my usual brand I used as it began to taste like clay. Losing my hair was devastating. I always prided myself with nice thick curly hair. To watch it slowly fall out was mentally painful both times. The loss of eyelashes is so much more than cosmetic; you have to deal with dust particles flying into your eyes after you lose them, and they actually poked my eyelids as they grew back. Meals that were at one time my favorites, no longer tasted as remembered. I didn't feel like me. I didn't look like me and I didn't recognize my world anymore. I would have moments of great sadness and others of happiness and hope. I never take anything for granted these days. I believe no matter where you are in your experience of cancer there continues to be life changes. From the time I plunged into the world of cancer I began to morph into another person. Stronger? Maybe. More accepting and less self- judging; Maybe. More determined to leave something worthwhile behind; definitely.

I have found one such change; how little things that may have brought me such irritation no longer do. For example when we moved to our house in Brighton, I must admit I was not happy. It was not my first choice. It didn't have a big shade tree in the back or a front porch to sit on to read a book or wave to our neighbors. It had a basement full of gambling machines (now what does that tell you?). This house did however, come with a built in swimming pool which overlooked a beautiful green common area complete with a little run off pond surrounded by trees. The pool, or cement pond as Jed Clampett from the Beverly Hillbillies would accurately describe it, was landscaped with rocks, large and small. I used to think the pool completely ruined the view in the back. All those rocks and that ugly metal fence! I stopped one day recently to take a look at the little weeds that popped up between the hard unforgiving rocks with their tiny colorful flowers and watched as little pollinators flew by or stopped to check out the nectar. It's amazing how nature works.

These days I enjoy the perennial flowers we have planted, and gaze at the blue pool water all summer long. In the winter we watch the squirrels try to find their buried nuts and scamper across the pool cover. I enjoy looking at the large billowy grasses that sway back and forth during all four seasons against that ugly fence. During the cold hard winter I will imagine hearing the loud, sometimes deafening spring song of the amazing little peeper frogs, which seem to magically come alive. The view didn't change, my perspective did.

At times I feel overwhelmed thinking I am helpless, the Cancer, our environment, the state of the world-all heavy rocks. But there are things I can do. I can vote for candidates who support my beliefs, on healthcare and the environment. I can attend rallies and marches that stand for a clean planet and freedom for all, not just a few. From the earth to my closet and cupboards I am able to help make positive waves of change. In 2019 consumer spending made up 69 percent of the US economy, which in dollar amounts equals a whopping $14.3 trillion. In our world where money talks and we listen, this is real power. So when we the consumers, decide enough is enough, we can make that shift from toxic and diseased to healthy and green. Knowing my choices do make a difference, I will continue to support renewable energy, small businesses like local mechanics, farmers that restore the soil, and resale stores that support healthy working conditions. I will continue to purchase Fair Trade and organic products, and of course purchase less, purging more.

A beautiful Monarch butterfly

...from basic rocks to
flamboyant flowers around
our pool...

Our radiant Rose of Sharon Busch

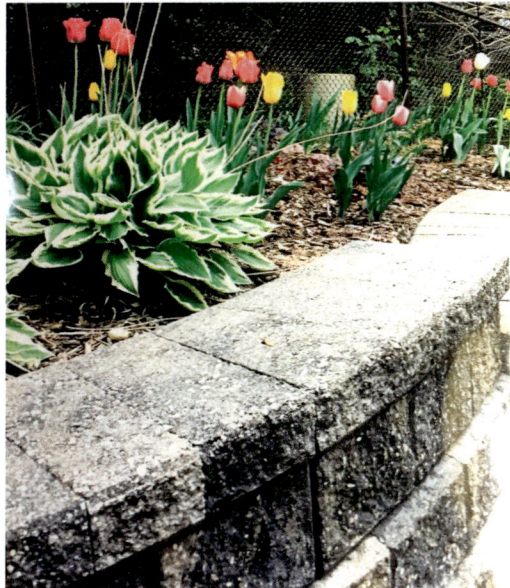

Tulips that brighten our spring

CHAPTER 20

Grab Your Moments

"Life is like an ice cream cone.
You have to lick it one day at a time"
Charles M. Schultz

I am feeling good these days. So good in fact that I went sky diving with Katie in July. She had planned to skydive when she turned 30 with a few of her College friends. However when the time actually came to jump, they were dropping like flies. (No pun intended) During one of her visits in Michigan she mumbled something about needing three people to join her in order to get a discount, so I blurted out "I'll go!" Smiling she asked "really?" I responded with an "Absolutely!" The experience was incredible, the view spectacular and memories sweet. What better way of celebrating Katie's Birthday. I remember her first sweet scream at her birth, and today her ear-piercing scream as she plunged from the plane!

I will continue to enjoy my life. No big expensive trips are needed for me. I'm happy taking walks in the nearby State park or cleaning out boxes in the basement. Lou, Ellie, and I registered for a squirt gun 5K. It was a perfect warm summer evening. We all got there early to pick up our runner's packet which consisted of a free t-shirt, candy, and not a little squirt gun, but big water soaker. We all smiled. This was going to be fun! A portion of the running route was thru a wooded area of a local park. It provided not only a nice shaded path, but the trees and bushes provided perfect hiding places for kids and adults alike to ambush and drench unsuspecting runners! You could hear squeals and laughter all along the route. We all enjoyed the run except Carly who complained about her beautiful fur coat getting wet. The next week Lou and I signed up for a bike ride that took us thru Green Field Village in Dearborn, MI. I love visiting this village. After a visit I really appreciate all our appliances and gadgets that make our lives so much easier in the 21 Century. We completed yet another half marathon at Disney World February of 2020. Lou had signed up along with Ellie's boyfriend to join in the run this time. I guess the boys thought Ellie and I just had too much fun last year or maybe they just wanted their own medals. We all enjoyed ourselves along the route taking in the fireworks and various Disney characters along the way. We followed the run with a visit to Coco Beach. Not only is this the popular beach along Florida's Space Coast, but it is also where an astronaut found a Jeanie bottle in the popular 1960's TV show "I Dream of Jeanie". Although I walked and searched the white sand, I could find no bottle with a Jeanie to grant me 3 wishes.

My bag of rocks seem lighter to me these days, not because I have forgotten or forgiven myself for the stupid things I have said or done, but rather I have put them into perspective. I now plan for but never assume I will have tomorrow. In so doing I feel lighter.

I have this last story I would like to share with you, taken from a book by Mark Levy entitled "If Only It Were True." He writes:

"Now imagine that you've won a contest, and your prize is that every morning a bank will open an account in your name containing eighty-six thousand four hundred dollars. And there are only two rules you must follow: The first rule is that everything you fail to spend is taken away from you that night. You can't cheat, you can't switch the unspent money to another account: you can only spend it. But when you wake next morning, and every morning after that, the bank opens

a new account for you, always eighty-six thousand four hundred dollars, for the day.

Rule number two: the bank can break off the game without warning. It can tell you at any time that it's over, that it's closing the account and there won't be another one. Now what would you do? It's very simple: every morning when you wake up, they give you eighty-six thousand four hundred dollars, on the sole condition that you spend it in one day. If you don't spend it all by the time you go to bed, you lose the unused balance." After Marc's character Arthur *thinks about it his friend Lauren explains "We all have that magic bank account: it's TIME. A big account filled with fleeting seconds. Every morning when we wake up, our account for the day is credited with eighty-six thousand four hundred seconds, and when we go to sleep every night, there's no carryover into the next day."*

I try not to forget Mr. Levy's game when I'm having a rough day.

As I finish writing this book, I have wrapped up multiple treatments. The professionals tell me it is just a matter of time before it will return. I choose to be positive these days hoping for more than less and take advantage of every extra minute I am given. I'll do what I can to make positive changes in this world and enjoy my time. After all we are born into this world to live the best life we can, collecting our bag of rocks as we go, always knowing our time here will come to an end, and another existence in the stars awaits us.

Katie and I strapped up and ready to jump

You cannot go through a single day without having an impact on the world around you. What you do makes a difference and you have to decide what kind of difference you want to make.

-Jane Goodall